adolescence

a guide for parents

Michael Carr-Gregg
& Erin Shale

Illustrations by Ron Tandberg

Vermilion
LONDON

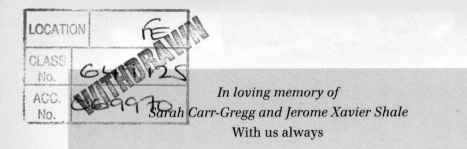
In loving memory of
Sarah Carr-Gregg and Jerome Xavier Shale
With us always

1 2 3 4 5 6 7 8 9 10

Copyright © 2003 Michael Carr-Gregg and Erin Shale

Michael Carr-Gregg and Erin Shale have asserted their moral right to be identified as the authors of this work in accordance with the Copyright, Design and Patents Act 1988.

First published in Australia and New Zealand in 2002 by Finch Publishing Limited

First published in the United Kingdom in 2003 by Vermilion, an imprint of Ebury Press
Random House UK Ltd. Random House, 20 Vauxhall Bridge Road, London SW1V 2SA

Random House Australia (Pty) Limited, 20 Alfred Street, Milsons Point, Sydney, New South Wales 2061, Australia

Random House New Zealand Limited, 18 Poland Road, Glenfield, Auckland 10, New Zealand

Random House (Pty) Limited, Endulini, 5A Jubilee Road, Parktown 2193, South Africa

Random House UK Limited Reg. No. 954009
www.randomhouse.co.uk
Papers used by Vermilion are natural, recyclable products
made from wood grown in sustainable forests.

A CIP catalogue record is available for this book from the British Library

ISBN: 0091891620

Printed and bound in Great Britain by Mackays of Chatham plc, Chatham, Kent

Edited by Bryony Cosgrove
Editorial assistance from Ella Martin
Text designed and typeset in Emona by Dizign
Illustrations by Ron Tandberg
Internal photos by Zoe Finch, Barnaby Norris and Briony Timmins

Notes   The 'Authors' notes' section at the back of this book contains useful additional information and references to quoted material in the text. Each reference is linked to the text by its relevant page number and an identifying line entry.

Disclaimer   While every care has been taken in researching and compiling the information in this book, it is in no way intended to replace professional medical advice and counselling. Parents are encouraged to seek such help as they deem necessary. The authors and the publisher specifically disclaim any and all liability arising from the use or application of any information contained in this book.

CONTENTS

Introduction   iv

1   **What is adolescence?**   1

2   **Early adolescence – 'Am I normal?'**   10

3   **Middle adolescence – 'Who am I?'**   31

4   **Late adolescence –
'What is my place in the world?'**   57

5   **The tasks of adolescence**   71

6   **The ideal environment for
raising an adolescent**   90

7   **Communication with adolescents**   119

8   **Relationships, sex and questioning
sexuality**   140

9   **In case of emergency**   155

10   **Frequently asked questions**   181

11   **Final words and over to you ...**   210

Acknowledgements   218

Helpful contacts   219

Authors' notes   220

Further reading   227

Index   230

The Miraculous Mood Meter   233

INTRODUCTION

Parenting adolescents is challenging, exciting and probably one of the most potentially rewarding tasks you will ever face. Most adolescents, however, rebel against their parents to some extent. It is the 'duty' of each new generation to educate and enlighten the previous one. Adolescents want excitement, they want thrills, and they are not always sensible. They want privacy, independence and adult status, sometimes without showing that they are capable of, or deserving of, any of this. Most of all, however, deep down they want the love, respect and acceptance of their families.

Many parents describe raising an adolescent as demanding, terrifying, exhausting and sanity-threatening. How often have you overheard comments such as 'Why don't teenagers come with a manual and operating instructions?', 'Nothing I do is right!' and 'I'm going crazy!'? Take heart. You are in excellent company. Raising adolescents today is a lot like trying to pick up mercury with a fork.

Recently, British Prime Minister Tony Blair declared that being a parent is tougher that being prime minister. When he adorned the front pages of newspapers across the world at that time, it was not because of some international crisis but because his oldest son, Euan Blair, had been arrested for being 'drunk and incapable' in London's Leicester Square after finishing his exams. Oh, to have been a fly on the wall in the Blair household that night. Even more recently, the nineteen-year-old twin daughters of US President George W. Bush, Jenna and Barbara Bush, also featured in the news, accused of trying to buy alcohol with someone else's identity card. The legal drinking age in Texas is twenty-one. It is comforting to know that even a prime minister and a president can have a few headaches with their offspring.

We decided to write *Adolescence* because we identified the need for a book to help take some of the fear out of parenting. Knowledge is power. Knowledge is also very reassuring. An overwhelming number of parents we have encountered in our counselling work are searching for that reassurance and for practical suggestions on how to best nurture the young people they care for so enormously: their children.

Many parents also find parenting a lonely business because they are afraid to share their concerns with other parents. Parenting need not be lonely. Often you simply need an opportunity to hear how other parents have approached similar situations, to relax and to laugh about it all. So, in addition to the insights we offer into adolescent behaviour, we have also included some reflections from other parents and, most importantly, from young people themselves. Major concerns such as adolescent moodiness, drugs, depression, sex, relationships, suicide and eating disorders are covered in detail.

Parents cannot be expected to have all of the answers all of the time. You cannot be expected to make the right decision the first time, every time. And you cannot do it all alone. What is important, however, is that you show your adolescents that you love them, that you are aware of what is possibly upsetting them and that you know some helpful

things to say and do. We also suggest what to avoid saying and doing. It is much easier to support young people if you are aware of the particular issues and 'tasks' facing them. In order to throw some light onto what can be a mystifying period, we will briefly outline the major stages of adolescent development and give practical suggestions to make life easier for all concerned.

In writing *Adolescence* we have tried to come as close as possible to providing 'The Book of Instructions' parents have long thought should come with each child. Parenting can and should be enjoyable once you come to grips with a few of the 'inside secrets' of adolescent development. There will be some hard times, trying times, but there are always ways to start over and to strengthen the precious relationship you have with your children. We outline practical and achievable strategies to help you build a more positive relationship with your adolescent. Armed with knowledge, strategies, determination and, most of all, love, you are off to a great start. We also recommend that you hold onto your sense of humour. Young people appreciate it when parents can loosen up and laugh when things don't exactly go to plan.

Parenting is the most important job in the world. You are intimately involved in the development and evolution of a unique individual. The guidance and support you can provide is priceless. Adolescents may only comprise a small percentage of our population, but they represent 100 percent of our future.

How can you get inside the seemingly complicated head of your adolescent? How can you best protect, nurture and love your adolescent? Read on.

Erin Shale
Michael Carr-Gregg

CHAPTER 1

What is adolescence?

The more parents understand the stages of adolescence and the issues facing young people at each stage, the better prepared they will be to respond sensitively and to offer appropriate support.

Adolescents come in three delicious flavours: early, middle and late. They begin their journey as children and complete it as young adults. Despite the

> The old believe everything, the middle-aged suspect everything, the young know everything.
>
> **Oscar Wilde**

pain along the way, it is a wonderful evolution. We will take you through the journey called adolescence and all of the various stages and tasks encountered. We recommend you bring a brown paper bag because sometimes the ride can be rough. Hang in there!

The stages of adolescence

It is important for parents to understand the stages of adolescence and to be prepared for what is coming. Knowing what is likely to happen in these stages will allow parents to better support their adolescents. In essence, young people face three big questions:

- In early adolescence, 'Am I normal?'
- In middle adolescence, 'Who am I?'
- In late adolescence, 'What is my place in the world?'

These questions, understandably, can be very daunting for young people. Be patient with them.

Remember your own adolescence

Adolescence is living proof that Mother Nature has a fabulous sense of humour. Often, everything we did to our parents when we were young is done to us! What goes around, comes around.

Do you remember when you were young? Many of us consciously or unconsciously choose to erase from our memories as much of our own adolescence as possible. It's a kind of parental amnesia. The next time you feel like selling your offspring into the slave market or running away from home, look a little closer and you may just glimpse an image that is horrifyingly familiar, amazingly similar to someone who accompanied you through your adolescence. Like father like son? Like mother like daughter?

If possible, talk over the concerns you have about your children with your own parents. Grandparents will often delight in reminiscing about how you behaved as an adolescent and the various 'escapades' you got up to. Grandparents are also well placed to comment upon the similarities between you as a child and adolescent, and your own children.

The situation becomes even more fascinating when parents debate whether a particular characteristic of their child has been inherited from the mother or the father. Parents love to take the credit for the positive personality traits of their children, but rarely rush forward to lay claim to being responsible for those less than desirable behaviours. This is where grandparents love to set the record straight by retelling those stories adults might prefer to forget about their own adolescence.

Grandparents have the advantage of both distance and experience and can offer valuable advice. They are often removed enough from the immediate 'battleground' to be able to offer an unbiased view, and have usually lived through similar situations with you as a teenager. Despite the enormous changes that have occurred in our world since the time we were teenagers, the fundamental truths do not change greatly, if at all. Grandparents, therefore, can provide reassurance that you will survive the inexplicable ups and downs of your children. They survived yours. You emerged a productive member of society. So, too, will your children.

If you are adamant that you were in no way as feral, in no way as obnoxious as your own child, this still won't rescue you from having to work out how to ensure the survival of yourself and your family over the next few years.

> Few things are more satisfying than seeing your children have teenagers of their own.
>
> **Doug Larson**

> Heredity is what sets the parents of a teenager wondering about each other.
>
> **Unknown**

The roller coaster ride

Think of adolescence as a bit of a roller coaster ride. Your entire world may begin to resemble a theme park unless you equip yourself with some up-to-date knowledge and survival strategies. (We hope you are not afraid of heights!)

Remember when we used to talk about the Terrible Teens? Whereas the roller coaster ride used to start when children turned thirteen and all concerned could breathe a sigh of relief and disembark from the ride when their offspring turned twenty, adolescence has changed. The time span that encompasses adolescence is changing. Research from both the United States and Great Britain shows that adolescents seem to be going through puberty earlier now than ever before; some as young as eight years old. And they are tending to leave home later than ever before. The average young person now leaves home somewhere between the ages of 25 and 28, and there are some who appear so comfortable that they may stay much longer. There are numerous reasons for this, the most common being the need for young people to remain at home due to the financial constraints of further study. If the length of the ride has increased, it is more important than ever to ensure you know the highs and lows to expect, and how to survive them.

During this roller coaster ride, adolescents undergo considerable emotional and physical changes. The physical changes you can see. If the emotional changes were visible, they would be even more dramatic than the physical ones. Every adolescent is unique. Some experience difficulties during one particular stage of adolescence, some through all stages and some sail relatively happily through it all. Sometimes, however, those who appear to be happy are simply very good at hiding their fears and uncertainties. The more parents understand the stages of adolescence and the issues facing young people at each stage, the better prepared they will be to respond sensitively and to offer appropriate support.

Adolescence at a glance

- An extended time of change, challenge and health risk with puberty starting earlier (as young as eight in some cases)
- A roller coaster ride from childhood to adulthood
- Nobody gets off the ride until it's over
- The length of the ride varies

Parenting ... A mum's perspective

"

Erin: With six teenagers at home, five boys and one girl, you must know a lot about adolescence, Sandy. How do you stay sane?

Sandy: Nothing prepares you for what might happen during adolescence! And I'm not sure how sane I still am. Sometimes my kids don't let on too much and I get really cross when I'm not happy with the way things are. I get annoyed, but I try to remember what I was like at their age and try to give them a bit of latitude. I try to remember that sometimes they're children and sometimes they're adults. One of the boys could be playing with Lego™ one minute and the next day he's strutting his stuff and his hormones are raging. It must be confusing for them! I've got rules but I try not to be dogmatic. Sometimes I think, Is it time to change the rules? It's a trying time. I really believe that what you do in the first five years comes back to you in the next fifteen.

Erin: So you think it's important to spend time with children when they are little?

Sandy: Definitely! From the time my kids were little we did everything together. It doesn't mean that you'll have no problems when they are teenagers, but it does help.

Erin: Can you give some idea of how you cope when things go wrong?

Sandy: Sometimes the only thing you can do is roll with them. I'll give you an example. Alan's fifteen, and recently he went out. I asked him to call me if he was going to be late. Well, I was wandering around the house at midnight thinking, If he's not already dead, I'll kill him! He got home *very* late! The next morning I asked him why he didn't call. 'There wasn't a phone,' he said. My only comment was, 'You know I worry!' You have to let them know how you feel, but there's no point in raging.

Erin: Do you let your teenagers know what you think about drugs and alcohol?

> Sandy: Absolutely! I tell all of my kids what I think. They know what I believe. I've done the best I could do bringing them up and I just keep talking to them.
> Erin: Do you think that talking is the most important thing?
> Sandy: Yes, but also I never put them down. I might say that what they're doing is stupid, but never that they are stupid. There's a big difference. I make sure we say 'Sorry'.
>
> **Erin**

It goes both ways

Saying 'Sorry' is an important response. Young people value justice, and a parent who is willing to express regret for what was said or done has a good chance of rebuilding and maintaining a relationship. This is not a 'face losing' exercise for the parent. If anything, it is allowing your adolescent to see that you are a real person with feelings, able to admit that you are not perfect. Young people detest the fact that their parents always have to be 'right'. Admittedly, many adolescents give the impression that they know everything and are never wrong. It's a bluff! Often they are actually scared and are feeling their way along each day. It is much easier for an adult to make the first move to say 'Sorry', and the payoff is usually fewer sleepless nights!

What is successful parenting?

- Slowing down and taking time to be with children as they grow up.
- Relating to young people, using their language – adolescent-friendly communication.
- Saying you care and showing you do.
- Being patient, supportive and willing to compromise.

> The average teenager still has all the faults his parents outgrew.
>
> **Unknown**

CRUNCH TIME

The messy house

Which is the most appropriate response if, after constant requests, your adolescents continue to leave clothes lying around the house?

- Tell them how hard you work and how unfair this is
- Make a bonfire and burn the clothes
- Put the clothes in a box, lock it away and make them wait a week to get the clothes back
- Appeal to their sense of fair play
- Pick the clothes up, fold them neatly and put them back in their rooms

Tell them how hard you work and how unfair this is

This kind of appeal rarely works. Young people don't respond positively to whingeing or the martyr routine. They simply switch off or hit back with one of the stock adolescent responses we've all heard at some point: 'I never asked you to work hard', or 'Don't blame me if you hate your job!'

Make a bonfire and burn the clothes

Wouldn't you just love to see their faces if you tried this! Sadly, that brief moment of 'triumph' would be just that, brief. You can kiss goodbye to any positive relationship you may have had with them. Your adolescents might respond in far more volatile ways than even you could imagine, and who knows where that could end. Have fun thinking about it … but don't do it!

Put the clothes in a box, lock it away and make them wait a week to get the clothes back

Great tactic to make your adolescents realise you are serious. Give a warning first, however. If you can involve your adolescents in a discussion about your feelings and the consequences if the behaviour continues, you have a much greater chance that this will be a successful strategy. You won't be seen as being unfair because your adolescents have had a warning and an opportunity to give their opinions. Don't back down on enforcing the consequences! Consistency is important in these situations.

Appeal to their sense of fair play

This rarely works, especially if it is presented as a lecture. You would at least have to indicate consequences to follow if the behaviour continues. Young people are impulsive, often don't think things through and need to be taught that behaviour does involve consequences.

Pick the clothes up, fold them neatly and put them back in your children's rooms

Do not get caught up in this pattern unless you want to spend every spare minute in the next twelve, thirteen or fifteen years being a slave for your adolescents. While at first glance this may appear to be a noble act of parental love, you are only teaching your adolescents to be irresponsible, thoughtless and selfish. Being a good parent does not mean you have to relinquish all of your rights as a person. Your adolescents deserve respect. So do you. Your adolescents deserve to be listened to. So do you. A good parent is fair but also expects fairness in return.

summary

What is adolescence?

- The three stages of adolescence are: early, middle and late
- The three big questions facing adolescents are: 'Am I normal?' 'Who am I?' and 'What is my place in the world?'
- Adolescents undergo dramatic physical and emotional changes
- Try to remember your own adolescence
- Adolescence is a roller coaster ride, and no-one gets off before it's over

CHAPTER 2

Early adolescence — 'Am I normal?'

Parents need to be aware that young people are usually not able to predict or easily 'control' their own feelings and emotions during this changeable period.

The major question for early adolescents is, 'Am I normal?' Working out the answer is a big issue for young people.

> It's difficult to decide whether growing pains are something teenagers have – or are.
>
> **Unknown**

Early adolescence is when most children hit puberty – a time of many physical changes. It is common for adolescents to lock themselves in the bathroom for hours, staring at every nook and cranny, every hair and lump. They can be found transfixed before a mirror, and it can be difficult to ascertain if they are delighted or horrified by what they see. Their bodies and emotions are changing at an alarming speed. They desperately want to be like their friends, to be 'normal'.

Apart from discussions at home, most children today receive detailed sex education at primary school, which usually continues into secondary school in health education, science or personal development classes. These classes cover physical and emotional changes associated with puberty, sexual intercourse, conception and contraception. Parents need to be involved in this important aspect of a young person's education. There are often opportunities for parents and children to attend information nights together. This is a time for parents to show interest and concern in their children while demonstrating an awareness that they are becoming more mature.

What is that gorgeous smell?

My son discovered deodorant last week. You've got no idea! The whole house smelled of it. It was just amazing. I walked in on him in the bathroom. 'Darling, you don't need that much. It only goes under your arms!' I closed the door, and turning to my husband, who had just come in, I said, 'Isn't that lovely. He said, "I love you Mum".' My husband looked at me and replied, 'Alice, he said, "Stuff you Mum!".' We laughed and laughed. Our little boy is growing up.

Alice, mum of an eleven-year-old boy

~~~ical changes at puberty

~~~growth slows down just before puberty hits. The calm before the storm perhaps. Apart from infant growth, physical changes occur more rapidly in adolescence than at any other time in life. During the adolescent growth spurt the heart doubles in size. And you thought your adolescent didn't have a heart! Some adolescents can grow up to 10 centimetres a year. It is not surprising that an adolescent can polish off a loaf of bread and an entire chicken for a 'snack' after school.

Some adolescents begin their growth spurt as early as nine while others begin as late as fifteen or sixteen. Levels of three types of hormones rapidly increase: gonadotropins, gonadal steroids and adrenal androgens (the names of the hormones that might be contributing to your headaches and those of your adolescent, too). Sexual organs mature, and puberty takes off.

A recent study revealed that of the 14 000 children surveyed, one in six girls reaches puberty by a staggering eight years of age compared to one in 100 just 25 years ago. (The start of menstruation can also trigger depression in young women. See Chapter 9 for more on adolescent depression.)

Emotional changes at puberty

While physical changes during adolescence can generally be seen, emotional changes are complex and often present parents with a greater challenge. Emotionally, adolescents are unpredictable. One day they can be stable emotionally and appear mature. The next they are suddenly very moody, tearful, angry and perhaps even immature in their responses to life. Parents need to be aware that young people are usually not able to predict or easily 'control' their own feelings and emotions during this changeable period. This is understandable when we consider the many physical and hormonal changes that also affect moods.

Branded early

I was sitting at my computer when my ten-year-old son approached and announced that he wanted a 'six pack'. Thinking that he was referring to alcoholic beverages, I looked at him in surprise and said, 'But, Rupert, you are far too young to drink beer.' He looked at me in exasperation. 'No, Dad. You know, the muscles.' He said this while pointing to a copy of a men's health magazine featuring a young man with a perfect set of muscles. This exchange illustrates something very interesting. When I was ten, I was oblivious to whether I had a six pack or wore the right brand shoes or T-shirt for that matter. What a contrast to the present day where my ten-year-old would not be seen dead without certain items of clothing. The marketers know this and target children, creating cravings that are hard for parents to ignore. One report in *Time* magazine said billions are spent annually on advertising directed at this section of the population. Many parents reported that they buy their children products they disapprove of or that may be bad for them because the children said they 'needed' the items to fit in with their friends.

Michael

Handle with care

Parents can assist enormously by simply being patient at this time and letting some things go. A young person who 'explodes' may simply be finding this confusing time too much to deal with on a particular day. The best reaction from parents may be no reaction. Allow 'time out' for the young person to be alone, and later inquire how things are going at school or with friends. Notice when a young person appears distressed and be prepared to try various approaches to offer support in difficult times. Often, if parents do allow an adolescent time to cool off, rather that reacting to an outburst or inappropriate language, all will go back to 'normal'.

Because adolescents are so sensitive to physical changes, these can result in emotional responses. Try to refrain from commenting upon obvious physical changes. A seemingly innocent remark can result in a negative reaction or a young person feeling even more anxious. In particular, comments about height and weight should be avoided as they can cause enormous concern for young people. It can be difficult to prevent a relative or the occasional visitor from making comments such as, 'My, haven't you grown', or, 'What a big girl you are now', but parents can ensure that *their* comments don't add to the angst their adolescents may be feeling. A good rule is to refrain from commenting upon physical changes unless they are guaranteed to elicit a positive response: 'If only I had your sporting ability. I would have given anything to be as athletic as you on the netball/cricket team.'

Why are physical changes occurring earlier?

There are three theories. Theory one says it is your fault. Yes, you the parents! You are feeding your children too well. Improved food and nutrition has been given some credit for this earlier onset of physical maturation, which occurs despite the amazing amount of junk food many adolescents consume in between meals. Theory two says it is the farmers' fault because too many growth hormones are being put into the food chain. Theory three, our favourite, says it is global warming, that there is essentially no difference between teenagers and tomatoes. If you keep them warm and feed them well, they will grow bigger.

It is possible, however, that researchers don't have a clue why this is happening. It is a concern, because it means adolescence is becoming more 'elastic'. Children are reaching puberty at a younger age, and are having to cope with mystifying changes to their physical and emotional selves as hormones rage through their bodies.

Implications of physical and emotional changes

Not only are young people reaching puberty earlier, but many are also becoming sexually active at an earlier age. Young people need to be aware of responsible behaviour and the consequences of sexual activity, and their parents need to know what their children are, or might be, doing.

Another consequence of reaching puberty earlier is that many young people question their sexuality much earlier than previous generations did. This can be a very worrying time for young people.

All of these changes may be contributing to the moodiness of many young adolescents. It is a confusing time, with much to absorb and adapt to. Being aware of why your adolescent may suddenly appear impossible to live with is important. Parents need to give their children 'space' and to be patient during what can be a rough part of the ride through adolescence.

In addition to early physical maturity, many young people are 'pushed' to grow up too quickly emotionally, especially through magazines, films and television. Unrealistic images may be presented of young people in relationships at an early age, so the pressure to find a boyfriend or girlfriend begins. Little wonder that many adolescents lock themselves in their rooms. For many, it's a scary world out there.

Keeping up appearances

Early adolescents are often teased about their appearance. It is a hot topic of conversation, considering the bodily explosions occurring almost daily. Appearance is immensely significant for young people, and parents need to be sensitive to this. Innocent comments can result in retaliation causing damage similar to that of a Scud missile.

Preoccupation with body size, shape and overall appearance can make some adolescents very unhappy with themselves. They can develop eating disorders such as anorexia nervosa and bulimia

The body stuff

" I remember seeing an early adolescent boy who was sent to me because he would not participate in any sport and was wagging school on sports days. He had become increasingly shy and withdrawn. Finally, he confided in me that he had a deformity he didn't want anyone to see. (His medical notes didn't mention any deformity.) He said that one of the bones in his chest stuck out in a grotesque way. He showed me the problem. His chest was perfectly normal, but he had convinced himself that it was abnormal and had become ashamed of it. I had a doctor reassure him that he was normal and the issue was resolved. It is not uncommon for young people to magnify these issues and become very anxious. Parents need to be vigilant. "

Michael

nervosa because of problems with body image. Parents can help to foster a strong sense of self-acceptance in young people by focusing on the positives. Encouraging adolescents to become involved in activities that give them a sense of achievement can increase self-esteem and take the major focus away from body size or shape.

Height variations are common around puberty, and adolescents who are significantly shorter or taller than their age group may experience some teasing or be treated as less or more 'grown-up' than other young people their age. These early and late maturers can at times be bullied, and parents need to look out for changes in behaviour such as an unwillingness to talk about school or go to school.

An additional disadvantage for early maturers is that taller adolescents are often expected to be more mature than other adolescents their age. Physical maturity is not necessarily accompanied by emotional maturity and this can place unnecessary stress on young people. Parents need to be aware of this if their children are taller than those in their age group. Each adolescent is an individual and will grow physically and mature emotionally at their own pace.

Physical and emotional changes in girls

The hormone estrogen increases more in girls during puberty and is responsible for height, muscle and bone growth, and development of the sexual organs. Girls generally experience a growth spurt before boys, some as early as nine. Other girls, however, begin to develop as late as fifteen.

The onset of menstruation can be unsettling for some girls, especially the premenstrual moodiness and tiredness many experience due to changing hormonal levels. Parents need to be sensitive to this, making some allowance for uncharacteristic behaviour while not drawing unwanted attention to what is happening.

Because many young adolescent girls look older than they are, they can sometimes find themselves in potentially unpleasant and even dangerous situations. A girl of fourteen might look nineteen or twenty and can attract attention she is unable to handle or respond to safely. This is a difficult area for parents and requires great sensitivity. It is not a good idea to simply forbid your daughter to go out or to tell her that she is inappropriately dressed (particularly if she buys her own clothes). Try to express your concern without angering, embarrassing or alienating her. A tactic that sometimes works is to refocus your concern on to others:

Becky: 'What do you think of this, Mum?' (Low-cut and extremely revealing outfit that makes fourteen-year-old Becky look twenty!)

Mum: 'You look great, but that outfit makes you look much older than you are. The problem is that you'll probably attract the attention of older guys, and things could be really difficult for you. They'll be expecting you to be really serious with them. It might not be much fun. It's a problem when you're too good-looking. What do you think?'

TANDBERG

Physical and emotional changes in boys

The hormone testosterone increases dramatically in boys during adolescence. It is responsible for the growth in the reproductive organs and muscles, height growth, a deepening of the voice and the appearance of facial hair. Most boys begin a growth spurt around the age of twelve, however some begin one or two years later.

The breaking of a boy's voice can be the cause of real embarrassment for some adolescents, and in this case the best reaction from parents is to not draw attention to it. Other boys, however, are proud of this change and are happy for their parents to acknowledge this event. Parents can help by not focusing attention on the unease boys may feel. Even something as straightforward as being fitted for a cricket protector can be an awkward procedure for an adolescent.

'Am I normal?' This is the question young people are asking themselves. Keep it in mind as we explore other hurdles adolescents must negotiate during this period.

Tracing the journey

The journey starts with but a single step ... then just one more, another, and another. How different the adolescent journey where each step optimistically engages the world around it. Helping children take steps that allow them to feel the joy of discovery and achievement builds a whole outlook on life and allows them to eventually take on the greatest challenges and cruellest adversities.

It starts early. On day one, if not before. Experiencing (not just 'learning') how to write a character of the alphabet, catch a ball, pat a cat, plant a flower, ride a bike, draw a line, talk to another person ... All these 'steps' help lay down those complex layers of emotionally tagged experiences that help form those life paradigms. Providing an atmosphere of love, trust and support, then spending the time to demonstrate strategies that build skills and experience, is among the more valuable things you can do for your children. And the sooner the better – although it's never too late to start. Consistency of approach lays down a 'way of going about life', like the steady hand on the tiller of a boat.

Of course, life is not all fun and laughter. Coping with frailty, bad luck and cruelty is just as important a lesson as any other. Being 'balanced' or 'grounded' is vital for children and teenagers. Feeling the security of the earth beneath their feet, while also enjoying the feeling of being able to soar on high – and come safely back to earth – as they must. For parents it may be hard to come to terms with the fact that it is their life, not yours. But the journey will be the richer for helping them enjoy theirs. Amazingly enough, most people (and children in particular) can innately sense genuine love and, if not too damaged by their world, can enjoy trust. And from that basis, they can explore and experience with enthusiasm.

**Dan Stojanovich,
father of Natasha, 20,
and Tania, 14**

TANDBERG

Hurdles facing a young adolescent

Young adolescents tend to hang out with a peer group of their own sex to test their psychological acceptability. They must resolve some important questions:

- 'Am I normal?'
- 'Do my peers like me?'
- 'Am I an okay person?'

This period generally coincides with the transition from primary to secondary school, which presents a host of exciting and terrifying challenges we look at a little later in this chapter.

Young adolescents also begin the normal breaking of childhood ties that bind them to their parents. They begin a journey through adolescence, and a magnificent thing happens. They seem to receive an instinctive and subtle push to begin breaking away. Something along the lines of bears waking from hibernation, salmon swimming upstream, birds leaving the nest. You have the picture!

I'm thinking ...

Adolescents become capable of abstract thinking at this stage. They begin to think in a more adult way. In other words, they develop the ability to manipulate all sorts of information (and people!) and to question. Does this sound familiar? You will be stopped in your tracks with the question, 'Why?'. You now have a person in your home who has suddenly realised that they have the ability to argue and even to reject a whole range of situations and processes previously accepted without much or any opposition. A complex chemical process causes the structure of the brain to change a little at puberty. Looked at positively, it is another sign that your child is becoming a young adult.

Early adolescence is a very exciting time because what it actually means is that our children look at us for the first time through adult eyes. The response is generally, 'Oh my God, look what I've got for parents! One, or maybe two intellectually challenged people who are chronically embarrassing, come from Planet Boring and who have been sent to make my life hell!' Wonderful stuff! They look at us, do a kind of mental vomit, and they move away – they are off on their journey, breaking childhood ties. Tremendous! We wouldn't want it any other way.

Experiencing loss and fear

Early adolescents face two daunting feelings:

- A sense of loss
- A sense of fear

These feelings are at the very core of each young person at a busy time in their lives.

A sense of loss is experienced by some, but not by all, adolescents. Previously, the mother and father they were closely bonded to could do no wrong. (Those were the days!) Now, in the highly critical eyes of a young adolescent, parents have been 'sprung', pinned down in a harsh spotlight, and the truth is out. Parents are not perfect after all. This shocking revelation, and the associated breaking-away process, creates a certain sense of sadness in young adolescents at a deep level.

Understandably, the second deep feeling in young adolescents, therefore, is fear. This is so carefully hidden by most adolescents that many parents don't even recognise its presence. Psychiatrist Sigmund Freud said that all fear was the fear of the unknown. Adolescents are heading out into the unknown. As adults, we have made this journey; we have travelled the rocky terrain. Adolescents' fear is perfectly reasonable, and yet wild horses couldn't drag this admission out of most of them. Furthermore, most adolescents are not even aware themselves that they are experiencing *fear*, let alone *loss*.

What are the implications of all of this? How do young people show sadness and fear? By being *angry* and *moody*. Sound familiar? The biggest mistake parents can make is to respond to what is happening on the surface: *the anger*. It is very important to look beyond and behind the behaviour to see what is really going on. Your adolescent hasn't become a monster overnight. He or she is simply struggling with some of the biggest issues and questions any of us probably ever face. 'Am I normal?' It's a frightening question for any person at any age. The desire to fit in and to be accepted never entirely leaves us, regardless of age. Wanting to belong and to be liked takes on an all-consuming importance for early adolescents. This can be a very worrying time for them, given the physical changes occurring and the fact that they are also adjusting to the transition from primary to secondary school.

Starting secondary school

Many parents assume that once their children are safely settled into secondary school, they can relax. The pressure is off. It's rarely so easy. The transition to secondary school for some adolescents can be as stressful as the first day starting school. It is important for parents to attend school functions at every opportunity and to be involved with their child's new school. Although the child may look more confident at this age, the expectations at secondary school can be daunting, and parental interest and involvement can make an enormous difference at this important milestone in a young person's life.

- Show a real interest in your child's school. Know more than the school's address. When looking for a secondary school, try to find one that welcomes the involvement of parents rather than making them feel excluded.
- Every day, make time to ask questions and to listen. You should be hearing accounts of all that is going on. If not, find out why. Be aware, however, that children are often tired and hungry when they first get home from school. Give them time to have a snack and gather their thoughts. 'How was your day?' can be a better opening than, 'What did you do at school today?'. The latter can elicit the response, 'Nothing.'

■ Does your child seem unhappy, worried or moody? Investigate. This could be a sign that they are being bullied. What is the school's policy on bullying?

■ Does your child have friends? If not, look for an activity or sport where young people with similar interests will be found.

■ Is the school workload too heavy? Can you help out with homework? Make time to chat about subjects being studied: 'What are you learning in History? What books are you reading for English?' (Perhaps you could read the books yourself and have a talk about them.) 'What's Geography like? What are you doing in Sport? Tell me about the teachers. Who is the best teacher? So, you're going on camp next week … that should be fun … what will you be doing at the camp?' Rent the video, record programs of relevance, cut out newspaper articles. Offer to read over your child's homework or give some help getting started.

■ If you notice that your child is interested in a particular topic – dinosaurs, frogs, volcanoes, violins – have a look through bookshops or a library to find a book on this topic. Help search for relevant websites.

■ If you realise that your child is having a miserable time in one particular subject, contact the teacher of that subject directly. This is almost always better than going 'to the top' because the teacher concerned will appreciate the opportunity to address the situation without involving others. Avoiding a confrontation with the teacher is in the interests of all concerned, and usually things can be sorted out amicably. Perhaps your child is worrying unnecessarily. Perhaps there is a problem with a particular subject and the teacher can suggest how to approach this. Whatever the reason, an open, friendly approach is best. If things don't go well with the teacher you approach, then go higher. Consult administration staff.

■ Let your child know that you are proud of them and your love will not be altered regardless of academic results, that you aren't the kind of parent who expects top marks and only top marks. This reassurance will relieve your child of unnecessary stress and they will generally perform better. Some students are so worried about letting their parents down that they give up. It's all too hard. If a child's best effort is never good enough, or if this is the perception they have, why bother? Make sure your child knows it's okay if they aren't the most academic student in the school.

- If your child is not academic and doesn't gain much satisfaction from school work, try to build on what they are good at or interested in. Sometimes, programs offered out of school time offer new and exciting outlets. Perhaps your child may be interested in taking up dance classes, kick boxing, tai chi or flower arranging. There are many relatively inexpensive short courses run by community groups. You can usually purchase secondhand musical instruments, sporting equipment, sewing machines or other handicraft tools, depending on the interests of your adolescent. Young people sometimes simply need a little encouragement to start what could become a whole new world of interest for them. If you can find something that gives your child a sense of achievement and something to look forward to, they will be much happier. Not being brilliant at academic work suddenly won't be the end of the world.

Discover their passions

In raising our two children, we have tried to provide opportunities for them to develop skills and interests, to discover their passions. From an early age, they attended music and movement classes and have continued to enjoy music. Jessica, now thirteen, played violin for a number of years, but her real passion is singing. She is in her school choir and the Australian Girls Choir. She loves to perform and has participated in numerous events such as Carols by Candlelight and the AFL Grand Final. This involvement has been wonderful for her on many levels. To make such a commitment requires her to be very organised. It also brings her into contact with other girls with a shared interest, thus giving her a network of friends. So, even if there are ripples in the bonds of friendship at school, she belongs to another friendship group. It's great for her self-esteem.

Our eleven-year-old son, Thomas, is an avid reader, a lover of sport both as a participant and spectator – even commentator, analyst and statistician – and a keen classical guitarist. Hopefully, when he hits the teenage years, his many interests will keep him as happy and directed as his sister is. We are firmly convinced that young people need to be passionate about something to extend them and to give them an additional sense of fulfilment, of belonging and of purpose.

Anne Marie and Mike Minear

Supporting your child during early adolescence

Early adolescence is not the most rebellious period for most young people. If parents put in the effort during this time, however, they may avoid a lot of angst later on. The time when your child starts secondary school is a great opportunity to talk things through and establish a relationship based on mutual trust and respect.

We have to do everything we can to reassure young adolescents that, yes, they are normal. Despite the complexity of what is going on in the mind, body and soul of an early adolescent, the major role for parents is deceptively simple: to make adolescents feel safe, valued and, above all, listened to. In doing so, we need to use language that does not trigger adolescent sensitivity to feeling 'controlled'.

While it's important to allow your children 'space' as they come to terms with physical and emotional changes they are encountering almost every day, this does not mean disappearing and leaving your children to sort things out alone. Work to keep communication channels open. Be prepared to ignore or pretend you don't hear certain muttered comments or notice certain unsavoury behaviour. Focus on the positives.

Are you listening?

Listen to young adolescents. When they test the waters with new opinions and thoughts, acknowledge these and remain calm, regardless of how outrageous they may be. Never ridicule them. Show a willingness to talk without pulling rank. One of the most common criticisms young people make is that their parents think they know everything and won't listen to the opinions of anyone else, especially not their children. You can avoid a lot of heartache and save a lot of crockery if you are prepared to listen and to acknowledge that your child is able to hold an opinion different from yours. You can agree to disagree or to discuss why certain opinions are put forward. Keep the conversation positive. Avoid the trap of seeing each conversation as a battleground. There doesn't have to be a 'winner'. Young people respect being respected. They know the difference between being really listened to and being simply tolerated. They spot a condescending look or comment at supersonic speed. Show that you will listen and respect opinions. This way you will maximise your chances of keeping most of your sanity, and some of your hair, as you accompany your children through adolescence.

Survival hints for early adolescence

- Become fully involved in the transition to the new school.
- Avoid comments about physical changes.
- Be prepared for moodiness and respond with sensitivity.
- Watch for signs of your adolescent withdrawing and talk things through.
- Help your adolescent develop interests to increase self-esteem.
- Focus on the positives.
- Don't be offended if your adolescent wants some distance from you.

Being involved

My parents are good. There're not really strict. They do stuff with us … my dad helps me make stuff. He's a carpenter. We make billy-carts and things and I go to motor car races with my dad. And sometimes I go to movies with my mum. Mum and Dad like the stuff we like. Mum likes the same movies as my two brothers and me. They're eleven and sixteen.

If I was upset about anything, I'd tell Mum and Dad. They're nice!

Raphael, 14

CRUNCH TIME

School blues

What should you do if your adolescent seems to hate school?

☐ Tell them to grow up and just do the work
☐ Explain they will end up a loser if they drop out of school, and throw in how much you have spent on school fees for extra effect
☐ Ignore these complaints because most children don't like school anyway
☐ Ask why and brainstorm for possible solutions

Tell them to grow up and just do the work

Young people hate being dismissed like this. Try to find out **why** school is hated so much. Adolescence is already a difficult time for young people, and it's important that they have some 'connection' with school. School is a large part of their young lives. Do some gentle and sensitive exploration to find out what is going on at school.

Explain they will end up a loser if they drop out of school and throw in how much you have spent on school fees for extra effect

This may only anger your adolescent and, once again, doesn't really help you find out what might be causing the unhappiness with school. There could be a real reason for concern. Using the word 'loser' may also increase the pressure to succeed – dangerous if a young person already feels they do not measure up to expectations.

Ignore these complaints because most children don't like school anyway

Never ignore anything that is upsetting young people. It is **not normal** for a young person to hate school. This could be a great opportunity for you to get on your adolescent's 'wavelength'. Showing real interest and concern can pay great dividends.

Ask why, and brainstorm for possible solutions

Yes! It is important to find out what is going wrong and to help out as much as you can. This will bring your adolescent 'on side' and show that you are interested in their life. Show that you **don't** have set expectations and **you won't withdraw your love** if your adolescent chooses to pursue a course or career you didn't quite have in mind. Give a clear message that the most important thing for you is the happiness of your children.

summary

Early adolescence at a glance

This is a time of:

- Immense physical changes
- Anxiety about appearance, body shape, growth, sexuality ('Am I normal?')
- Teasing about appearance
- Same-sex friends
- Moving from primary to secondary school
- Breaking of childhood ties
- More adult thought processes

CHAPTER 3

Middle adolescence — 'Who am I?'

At this middle stage of the journey, the single most important thing for adolescents is their friends.

If the big question in early adolescence is 'Am I normal?', in middle adolescence it becomes, 'Who am I?'

> Don't laugh at a youth for his affectations; he is only trying on one face after another to find a face of his own.
>
> **Logan Pearsall Smith**

Many adolescents want to go out there to explore and find the answer for themselves. They do not want to be *told* what to do, how to behave, and they certainly do not want the answers served up on a silver platter. While parents often appear to have less direct influence over their adolescents at this stage, it is still possible to maintain a subtle influence. The most effective way to achieve this is to keep the communication channels open and to keep conversations focused on the positives.

We need to see for ourselves

Being fifteen sucks. You're in between. You're inferior. Your parents don't care much about you because your sister's in Year 12, and your brother's eight years old. You're always overlooked, underestimated. Yet, you're the liveliest of all your siblings. You grasp opportunities at school, you play sport, and you go by the rules. But no, oh no, to parents, a fifteen-year-old must be kept at home. Away from violence, drugs, away from the 'bad' people, the 'bad' kids. Little do they know, however, for a fifteen-year-old, the time is ripe to go and explore, and make decisions for yourself. How are we meant to instantly decide what is right or wrong unless we actually go out there and see for ourselves?

Robbie, 15

What to expect during middle adolescence

- Friendships become immensely important – parents less important
- 'Interesting' times during struggles with identity formation
- Rejection of adults and adult control
- Possible rebellious behaviour and communication breakdown
- Risk-taking behaviour
- Growing need for a 'guide' or mentor

The importance of friendships

The further adolescents go on this ride called adolescence, the *more* influence their friends will have. At this middle stage of the journey, the single most important thing for adolescents is their *friends*. At no other time in life is the desire to be with a peer group so strong. It is like an addiction. Family and even previously cherished pets cannot compete with the allure of the friendship group. This shift of focus from family to peers is not necessarily a bad thing, although try convincing the family dog to accept this.

One of the great risk factors that has been identified for drug misuse is adolescents having plenty of time on their hands, and 'hanging out' with other young people who have favourable attitudes towards drug misuse. While you can't choose your adolescent's friends, and it is never a good idea to forbid (a dangerous word to use with an adolescent!) association with certain friends, you can use some indirect influence.

Parents and friends

Have you heard the expression, 'If you can't say anything nice, don't say anything at all.'? This does not mean you will be left with nothing to say to your children until they have emerged from adolescence. And it should not mean there is nothing nice you can find to say about their friends. There must be something! Never use put-downs. Negative comments will generally only cause adolescents to become defensive and to associate even more closely with the dreaded friends.

What might work? Calm and subtle comments are a good start. Parents should not be afraid to voice their opinions about friends, especially if these are expressed in sensitive comments about behaviour that is not appreciated, rather than labelling the friends themselves as unlikable. It is important to also allow adolescents to express their opinions. Listen carefully to these. Talking things through rationally can sometimes result in an adolescent making up their own mind that certain behaviour and friends are undesirable. Resist the temptation to verbally assassinate the friends you believe have led your adolescent astray. This is like waving the proverbial red rag at a bull.

You are not obliged to love the friends of your adolescent. It is, however, a good idea to make them welcome in your home. If you won't have them around, chances are you will not see much of your own child while the friendship lasts. Adolescents desperately want to be treated like adults, and allowing them to invite friends over is a part of this. Show some trust in your adolescent. Good taste will generally prevail ... eventually! Friends come and go, so you don't want to alienate yourself from your adolescent because of the current friendship group.

Searching for an identity

Searching for an identity is one of the most important tasks facing an adolescent. This is where the roller coaster ride seems to become a little crazier and the appearance of your adolescent can change dramatically from day to day. There may be times when you won't be sure which version of your adolescent will turn up for meals, and the anticipation can be a killer! Green hair, blue hair, rings here-there-everywhere, black everything, striped hair, spiked hair, no hair. *No* hair!? This is when you could sell tickets to *Guess Who's Coming to Dinner?* at your place, and almost always be sure of an exotic floor show. You can also expect the music, language, jewellery – just about everything visible and audible – to change, again and again. These are the days when just as you think you've seen and heard everything, your adolescent will surprise you yet again.

Humour and quality time

I love spending time with my three daughters and being a part of their life. I am anxious that one day when they leave home, I won't have shared enough

of their life. It doesn't last forever so I relish every experience we share. And they keep me young. We often laugh together and that's important. One activity we all particularly love is playing the card game *Pictionary*. We have so much fun that the girls run to get the cards and we settle in for a really good night.

We laugh over other things too. Like occasionally when I get dressed to go out, they say, 'Mum, you look so daggy. Go and take that off, Mum.' They'll sometimes look at my shoes and say, 'You're going to wear those!?' This is accompanied by lots of laughter from all of us, even me. If I criticise what they wear, it's a different story though.

Androula Michaels, mother of three girls

Some adolescents do not readily find an identity. In order to discover *who* they are, they try on one mask after the other to find the one that fits. Many adolescents align themselves with 'groups' or 'cultures' to give themselves something to fit in with, something to belong to. There are the Goths, the Rappers, the Punks, the Ravers, the Homies, and they all have their own rules and regulations, their own music, clothes and icons. They are fascinating, modern-day equivalents of the Mods and the Rockers and Shakers from the 'olden days'. Playing with various identities is *completely normal*.

Clothes are an outward display of fraternity, a way of saying 'I belong', and belonging and acceptance are very important for young people. Every generation has its special 'brand' or 'badge' of membership. As adults we often choose to forget what we wore and did when we were adolescents. If the attire has become more outrageous, let's put that down to the amazingly creative imaginations of youth today. It's obviously getting harder and harder to find a new outfit to shock, a new 'uniform' to wear, a new statement to make that will be different from those of previous generations. Let's simply give young people credit for their creativity and sit back and enjoy the show. This is all just another part of finding the answer to that elusive question, 'Who am I?'.

All the kids wear them

Recently, I was browsing through a clothing shop, looking for some presents for my nieces and nephews when I overheard a conversation between a mother and her son of about thirteen.

Mother: (Casual, friendly tone, no sarcasm) 'So, let's see these pants you so desperately want.'

Son: (Reaches out and excitedly grabs a pair of baggy 'dance pants') 'These are the ones!'

Mother: (Holding the offending pants out at arm's length as if they were contaminated) 'You're joking! They're the ugliest-looking pair of pants I've ever seen! Why on earth would you want these?'

Son: (Visibly crushed and embarrassed, apologetic voice) 'All the kids wear them, Mum.'

Mother: 'They're awful. Look at the material. But if you really want them ...'

Son: 'It doesn't matter. It doesn't matter.'

Mother: 'No, you want them. Try them on. I suppose they might look better on.'

Son: 'I've changed my mind, Mum. Let's go.'

I certainly won't forget the heart-wrenching look on that young boy's face. Does it matter if a parent dislikes a particular item of clothing? The mother seemed completely unaware of the excitement and anticipation on her son's face, and was also unable to fully appreciate the level of disappointment her comments had produced. I don't know if the pants were purchased or not. Either way, I bet they will always have negative connotations for that young person.

Erin

Parents and the search for identity

As a parent, how should you react to these signs that your adolescent is searching for a comfortable identity? Pretending it's not happening is one option, though a difficult one to stick to. If you do feel compelled to make any comments on hair and clothing, make them positive. Be creative! Apart from ornaments that could actually be health threats, such as those inserted via body piercing, does it matter what shade your adolescent's hair is, or what adorns their body? ***Do not allow 'fashion' to alienate you from your adolescent.*** That is still your child under all the hair, jewellery and paint.

The main focus should be on your adolescent's happiness, and if a bottle of dye or a tin hat for that matter can contribute to the wellbeing of a young person, so be it. Who cares what the neighbours think? They could be enjoying the colourful comings and goings for all you know. Adolescents are very fragile and volatile when it comes to criticisms about appearance. If the colour of your adolescent's hair is the worst thing that happens to you during this roller coaster journey, you're laughing!

Misunderstood

> In a school corridor I spotted one of my students looking particularly unhappy …

Erin: 'Smile, Chris! By the way, I love your new haircut.' (Always be honest. Adolescents have an uncanny ability to spot insincerity. I really did like the hair)

Chris: 'Thanks!' (Brief smile) 'I'm getting in heaps of trouble over it, especially from Mum!'

Erin: 'What happened?'

Chris: 'I wanted to surprise her with my hair. She freaked out! I copped it so bad! She says I'm a menace to society.' (I had to restrain myself from bursting into laughter because Chris is anything but a potential menace. A fine student, but emotionally up and down like most adolescents)

Erin: 'Are you sure she wasn't joking?'

Chris: 'I don't think so. She says it a lot ...' (Despondent look)

Erin: 'I bet she's joking. Does she know you're one of my best English students? I think you're great! You're not a menace to anyone. You know, parents sometimes say things they don't really mean. She'll get over the hair. Give her time. Perhaps warn her next time though.'

A few days later ... corridor again. (Lots of teachers 'counsel' in corridors)

Chris: 'Hi Miss!' (Big smile!)

Erin: 'How's it going, Chris? Is society safe today?'

Chris: 'Maybe.' (Bigger smile) 'I told Mum what you said.'

Erin: 'Which bit?' (Oh no!)

Chris: 'I told her *you* think I'm *great* and I'm *not* a menace. Then I told her you said I'm your best student, you *love* my haircut, and she should just *get over it*!'

Erin: 'You're kidding! What did she say?' (Heart rate increasing by the minute)

Chris: 'She laughed a lot and she said she wants to meet you. And she said you're right. The "menace to society" thing is a joke. Most of the time anyway!'

Erin

It's funny the way a parent's raised eyebrow can do more damage to your psyche than, say, Chinese water torture.

Arabella Weir

TANDBERG

Rejecting adult control and support

A common aspect of many middle adolescents' search to find out who they are is the simultaneous spurning of adult control and support. Adolescents appear to want to challenge everything, especially parents and other authority figures. Teachers frequently speak of middle adolescents in either hushed or heated tones. This is one of the most difficult times in the adolescent journey for many parents, and a whole range of strategies may need to be tested and tried. It is at this stage that relationships with adolescents can become most strained, so parents need to proceed with caution.

The roughness of this patch will vary depending on the particular *temperament* of your adolescent and on *how you react* to each situation of possible conflict. Within a family, one adolescent can be calm and relatively easy to communicate with and the next very volatile and a nightmare to deal with. Parents are the experts on their children and are best able to tune into what upsets them. A strategy that works with one adolescent may not work with another. Parents need to consider various approaches to each situation and to work out the best approach for a particular situation. It can be trial and error, but it is important to keep trying.

Unique and special

My wife and I are very involved with our three children. We are constantly monitoring their responses to the world around them. Our son Andrew was fine until he turned eight or nine and he became very self-conscious about his weight. He's now eleven. He's always been a very sensitive kid. Hypersensitive. He's also extraordinarily kind in his attitude to his friends. I get very upset when he is emotional. 'The world sucks,' he says. 'I don't like the way things are happening.' These are tough things to hear from an eleven-year-old. I'm not very good at dealing with all of this but I give him lots of hugs and lots of reassurance. He likes that physical reassurance enormously. I always tell him he's the best kid ever. I was driving him to his piano exam a few weeks ago. He told me he felt very pressured about the outcome of the exam. 'Andy, it doesn't matter how you go,' I remember saying. 'No, it matters,' he replied. 'I might not get a high mark.' 'Not a problem,' I tried to reassure him. I think this made him feel better. He needs a huge amount of attention. Constant reassurance. I think all children are dependent on parental approval.

Our daughter, Angela, is a lot more resilient, though. She did go through a period when she was excluded by her peers. She came to us about it because we have always encouraged the children to talk to us. We never stopped telling her how great we thought she was. I encouraged her to focus on her studies and it worked. She got through this period, became one of the top students and started to feel good about herself again. During the bad period she walked around hunched up like she was in a cocoon. She's so different now. 'Dad, lay off,' she says. And I love it when she says, 'Dad, you're wrong you know.'

Our youngest, seven-year-old Jason, is very different from both the older children. He's very well adjusted. Confident. Doesn't give a shit about anything. The other day he came up to me saying he wants to have a permanent tattoo on his forehead. The word 'permanent' was emphasised. At the moment he has a temporary one. 'It's going to hurt,' I said calmly. 'Will it bleed?' Jason asked. 'It will bleed a bit.' I left it at that and he walked away. I'm hoping that's it, end of story. I live in hope.

Peter

How should parents respond to being rejected and challenged?

Maintaining positive communication will help enormously as will continuing to listen and respecting differences of opinion you may have with your adolescent. This does not mean you are unable to set rules of behaviour for your adolescent, but at all times attempt to *negotiate* these calmly rather than imposing them in a fit of rage.

Some common behaviour patterns in middle adolescence

While each adolescent is a unique individual, there are some common behaviour patterns parents may encounter during middle adolescence. Some parents tell you their son or daughter is an angel and you just want to stab them through the heart. Some adolescents shut down communication completely and parents are left in a kind of vacuum. This can last from 36 to 72 months, if you are really unlucky, and you begin to think, *What* have I got at home? Silence can be just as annoying as noise. As a variation on this, some adolescents develop a caveman-style monosyllabic grunt. Others perfect the ability to talk out of the side of the mouth, giving the impression that you barely exist. (It's an act. They still need you!) Some adolescents will tell you what you need to know but not much more.

Stay connected

Whatever the 'type' of adolescent you suddenly find inhabiting your house, the fact that most push parents and authority figures away is a positive sign. It seems to be nature's way of helping these young people to develop their independence, which they need to function as healthy adults.

While all adolescents are individuals and often vary their behaviour from day to day, a golden rule is to always approach a young person with a calm and open mind. Showing a willingness to listen and to acknowledge the feelings and opinions of a young person is a great start to establishing and maintaining a positive 'connection'.

Adolescents who have an outgoing temperament may be less affected by the emotional and physical changes happening to them. Be aware, however, that many adolescents put on a brave face while still feeling quite worried about all that is happening to them. This is an important time for parents to be very observant and to keep communication channels open.

There will be good days and bad days but the message to a young person should always be that they are a valued member of the family. There will be times when this will require patience, the willingness to compromise, and sometimes even 'lose' a few skirmishes.

Seen any good movies lately?

Surprise your adolescent (and perhaps yourself) by going along to see a movie you have heard them rave about. Ask questions about the lead actors, the music. Improvise! Get a conversation going and show you are interested in the things your adolescent enjoys. The same technique also works with books, sport and so on. Adolescents are a very suspicious lot so be ready for questions as to *why* you want to see a particular movie:

Parent: 'I went to see movie X today.'
Adolescent: 'You're kidding! What for?'
Parent: 'You've been saying how great it was and I felt like seeing a good movie.'
Adolescent: 'So did you like it?'
Parent: 'It was really interesting! I thought the music was great! Do you know anything about the soundtrack?'
Adolescent: 'Yeah, it's …'

And off you go!

Risk-taking behaviour

Most adolescents engage in risk-taking behaviour from time to time. *Such activities are a normal and essential part of growing up*. This testing of the world helps young people to define and develop their identity and underlines the separation that is occurring between them and their parents.

Risk taking, therefore, is not necessarily bad. Some forms of risk taking are valuable for adolescents: low risk taking such as playing sport, debating, volunteering, music or giving vent to creative abilities. All of this can have a positive impact not just on an adolescent's search for identity, but can also increase self-esteem. It is a positive way for adolescents to gently break their emotional dependence on adult carers while assisting them in forming meaningful relationships with their peer group. Parents need to be patient and to support their children through this experimenting with new experiences.

When you were their age

My parents seemed to have never forgotten the things that in their own childhood and teenage years upset or annoyed them. My siblings and I grew up knowing that any predicament we dug ourselves into, or decision we made, would be calmly discussed and wholeheartedly supported. Our relationship is such that they trust me and my siblings, so we do not have to lie to them. I think the reason I get along so well with my parents is that they never distanced themselves too far from their growing up, always remembering their desires to experiment, the magnetism of rebellion and the need for a certain amount of independence.

Anna Kelsey-Sugg, 19

TANDBERG

Healthy risk taking

Healthy risk taking is a positive tool in an adolescent's life for discovering, developing and consolidating identity. It is important to remember that learning how to assess risks is a process that we work on throughout our lives. Children and adolescents need support and practice in order to learn how to do this. Young children give clues about how they do or don't take risks. How eager are they to ride a bike or skateboard? How eager or reluctant are they to jump into deep water? Parents of adolescents may already have a good idea of how much of a risk taker their adolescent is likely to be by remembering past behaviour. Is this young person generally a cautious risk taker, a middle-of-the-roader, an adventurer or high-end risk taker, or a young person whose risk taking increases when with peers? Being aware of the 'type' of risk taker your adolescent may be will alert you to possible ways to help them.

Rather than seeing adolescent risk taking as an angry power struggle with parents, as rebellion, it is more useful to redefine it as a potentially helpful *testing process*. Through the taking of challenges and risks, adolescents find out *who* they are and establish *what* they will become. It is all a part of discovering the answer to 'Who am I?'. Without such life experimentation, our sons and daughters would never get on their bicycle, or take that first plunge into the water.

From dependence to independence

Of the many theories about child rearing, I favour those that emphasise the importance of the first three years of life to the subsequent development and progression of an individual through life. We focused much attention and time on both our daughters in their early years. As a consequence we were in tune with their idiosyncrasies and particular needs. Being in touch makes it easier to set limits while allowing the child freedom to explore and learn about the world. Natasha was a particularly exploratory child with a relentless curiosity that frequently took her outside the defined boundaries – the fishpond was a favourite spot. We adopted an approach that focused on minimising risk and *not fussing too much over battles that did not really matter. Structural change to the child's environment in the interests of safety works well. We installed an iron mesh over the fishpond. I think this principle of focusing on harm minimisation when setting limits is a useful approach at all stages of the child's development.*

From infancy through to adolescence, children need to make a gradual transition from dependence to independence in preparation for adult life. To do this they need to feel the exhilaration of risk in a stepped, graduated fashion, swinging away from the parent in ever-increasing arcs. Allowing some freedom to move encourages children to take responsibility for the consequences of their actions.

Parenting a child frequently challenges the parent to grow. Children are more likely to behave as they see their parents behave, rather than in response to what they tell them to do, especially if there is a discrepancy between the words and the actions. The parent needs to earn the respect of the child. I've attempted to be open and authentic with my children – warts and all.

As busy parents both engaged in a number of activities other than child rearing, we have aimed to allow time and space to be available and have fun with each of our daughters. Listening, good quality communication and trust are important to any relationship and in particular to the relationship of the parent with the developing child through to adolescence.

I have found the experience of parenting exquisitely painful at times; however, one of the most profoundly meaningful experiences of my life. Our daughters are flourishing. They are both mature, independent young women actively engaged in life. What better gift could a parent have?

Nan Presswell, mother of Natasha, 20, and Tania,14

Most parents are not overly concerned with low risk taking. Although often visually alarming, it is generally harmless. Watching young people skateboard can be a nerve-racking experience for parents but it is a far cry from the nightmare of high risk-taking behaviour: binge drinking, reckless driving, illicit drug use, smoking, train surfing, deliberate self-harm.

Sniffing out high risk taking

A recent, but potentially deadly form of high risk taking among adolescents is the sniffing of various household products. Children as young as nine or ten have been inhaling substances such as glue, paint, petrol, liquid paper, deodorant, insect spray and other aerosol products. A national survey completed in May 2001 by the Australian Institute of Health and Welfare found that one in three twelve-year-olds has experimented with paint- or glue-sniffing. Young people can become intoxicated on these substances, which are inexpensive and readily available. Once 'spaced out', they are more likely to engage in serious forms of life-threatening behaviour.

Parents need to be open with their children and to discuss the serious health effects of such behaviour. Many young people are unaware of the potential dangers of sniffing. These can include disorientation, nausea, vomiting, eye irritations, mood swings, aggression, eating disorders, unconsciousness, headaches and diarrhoea. Long-term effects can include damage to brain cells, the heart, kidneys and the oxygen-carrying capacity of the blood. It can also damage the respiratory system and lead to weight loss, hand tremors, muscle fatigue and even death. Be aware of where your children are and whether or not they appear to be happy or unhappy. Young people who know they are loved and important to the family are less likely to seek out dangerous risk taking.

Responding to risk-taking behaviour

High risk-taking behaviour can't be ignored. Sometimes parents inadvertently create a culture of entitlement where they hesitate to use moral language or to set limits or boundaries for their children. Do not shy away from raising the subject of risk-taking behaviour. The manner in which you respond, however, is crucial. Here are a few suggestions:

▓ Attempt to remain calm and try to initiate a reasonable discussion with your adolescent. Teenage television can be a great way to open up a discussion about various issues while also showing that you are interested in the life of your adolescent.

- Explain to your adolescent that you are worried because you love them.
- Avoid statements like, 'How could you be so stupid?' or 'Why are you throwing your life away?'. And definitely not, 'What are you trying to prove?'. Adolescents are often simply making a statement that they want to be noticed. It's worked, especially if you blast them. This only gives them another reason to push you away.
- *Notice* your adolescent. Notice the positives and ignore the negatives if at all possible. Show your interest in the friends, the music and everything that is important to them.
- Make an effort to show your adolescent that you *trust* them. Provide subtle opportunities for this. Often adults presume the worst from adolescents, and guess what they get? Reverse this pattern and you may be surprised. If shown trust and given real responsibility, adolescents do 'measure up' well. And, if your adolescent doesn't measure up the first time, say how you feel in a positive way and give them another opportunity. (It is a good idea to begin giving young children opportunities to show they can be trusted *before* they jump on the adolescent roller coaster.)
- Encourage your adolescent to become involved in fun and challenging activities. An active and busy adolescent is less likely to be bored and unhappy and less likely to take the dangerous risks. Adolescents do need ways to prove themselves. Help them to find safe ways to show their individuality. Providing opportunities for adolescents to receive their adrenaline rush in safe and constructive ways is critical. Sports and outdoor adventure camps provide opportunities for adolescents to put themselves 'out there'. Parents can help by providing and encouraging these types of fun and challenging activities.
- The *temperament* of your adolescent must be taken into consideration. Every young person is born with a particular disposition, which can impact on the nature and extent of the risk-taking behaviour engaged in. Some adolescents have a thrill-seeking

or sensation-seeking inclination, which makes them particularly attracted to the more perilous forms of experimentation. It is important to recognise this characteristic in adolescents and to parent accordingly. ***Whatever their temperament, it is beneficial to keep all adolescents busy.***

If we accept that risk taking is a normal and healthy part of adolescence, then society's main challenge is not to stop young people from experimenting with life but to protect them from life-threatening experimentation. Redirecting the energy and drive adolescents have into healthy and safer pathways allows the successful transition from the ***dependence*** of childhood to the ***independence*** of young adulthood.

Busy is best

My eldest grandchildren are sixteen-year-old identical twin girls, Lauren and Katrina. They have virtually been trouble-free teenagers for their parents. I think this is because their mother encouraged them to be involved in Little Athletics when they were younger. It was fun, instructive and healthy. As teenagers, they have continued their great interest in sport with netball, tennis and swimming.

They have also developed a very good attitude. They're competitive, but in the respect that winning isn't the be-all and end-all. Sport is great for kids because they learn to lose. You get the knocks but you learn how to handle them and how to overcome them early on. Lauren and Katrina love their sport and they're also meeting other people outside the school. That's terribly important. It's so important that parents don't just drop their children off at activities and think, 'That's that'. Children really want their parents there to watch them. The twins' parents go to see them play sport as often as they can and I go with their other grandmother too. It doesn't matter if the children have a major part or a small one. It's all about encouragement and showing that you're interested. The twins are always busy. Apart from sport, they also have a lot of other interests like their church group, and part-time jobs in the holidays. Trouble will always be around but you won't find it if you haven't got time to go looking for it.

 **Meg Robinson**

Causes of high risk taking

Some adolescents engage in high risk taking because they are bored, feel angry, and want to get your attention. More importantly, research has shown that the difference between young people who engage in risk taking and those who engage in *high* risk taking is *connectedness*. This is a feeling of belonging, of being important to some other person or persons, especially the family.

Connectedness seems to be a by-product of those families who strive to reinforce the value of being together and who communicate a sense of obligation to each other. In such families, an adolescent feels *safe*, and family members make time to have fun together, and create rituals and traditions. Such families try to be consistent and predictable while communicating a message that each family member and their feelings are important. If your adolescent feels a real bond with the family and considers themself to be a valued and loved member of the family, they are much more likely to avoid high risk taking. (This essential area of connectedness is covered in more detail in Chapter 5.)

Why all the anger?

- Feelings on the surface are often only a cover for the more tender feelings below. It's easier to be angry rather than sad or frightened.
- Underneath the anger (either ours or our adolescent's) we often find hurt, guilt, sadness or fear.
- Anger is often the 'safe' option that adolescents fall back on when they are overwhelmed.
- All adolescents have to learn to separate from their families – anger creates distance.
- Distance is achieved through 'acting out' behaviour or sullen monosyllabic communication.

It's tough being young

Maybe it's inevitable that only the occasional parent communicates effectively with their fifteen-year-old child. Just listening would be nice. Dropping the superior facade and the underestimating attitude would also do a lot towards eliminating the frustration we often feel.

Age is nothing. It should be the lowest priority for consideration. So many times, the aggravation caused by people telling me I can't do something because of my numerical age pushes me almost over the edge. A number cannot show the depth of my thoughts, the relevance of my feelings, and the correctness of my philosophies. The younger we are, the lesser our ability, in words, to express sensations. But we do feel essentially the same things.

Yanlo Yue, 15

Trusting and listening

Young people desperately want to be listened to and to be shown they are important. They are capable of great things, and perhaps parents need to focus less on 'age' and learn to trust their adolescents.

Young people learn to listen when parents listen to them. They also learn to trust when they are given responsibility. They will only learn to 'switch off' if their opinions are ignored. There is so much to be gained if parents communicate with their adolescents and respect their feelings and opinions. So much unnecessary frustration, so many angry clashes and misunderstandings could be avoided. It is very important to listen.

TANDBERG

The need for a guide

During this period of middle adolescence, your child needs at least one special person who can help nourish their uniqueness and provide some much needed **stability and security** in what is a rapidly changing and often insecure time. This special person can be a parent but more often is a teacher, a family friend or another trusted person. The presence of a least one **significant other**, who makes the adolescent feel valued, can make the world of difference to an adolescent. This person can be instrumental in discouraging high risk taking and encouraging feelings of self-worth in your child. Parents should not feel threatened if they are not the significant other. This is simply another aspect of an adolescent's need to break away from their parents, to establish independence and to become an adult.

Survival hints for middle adolescence

- Work to keep communication channels open.
- Listen to your adolescent and try to remain calm and positive regardless of the issue. Always allow your adolescent to express an opinion and to hold an opinion that may differ from yours.
- Don't be afraid to present your views but avoid criticisms, especially of friends, clothes, hair, music.
- Don't ban friends from coming over. Always attempt to explain why you feel the way you do and what behaviour you would prefer. Focus on the positives: 'I like John and he's got a real sense of humour but I'd prefer that he doesn't repair his bike on our Persian carpet again. It means a lot to me and I've been really upset about the mess.' A better approach than: 'Tell that idiot friend of yours that he's not welcome in this house ever again! He's a moron!'
- Avoid the words 'forbid' and 'banned'. Try to talk things through. Discuss, listen, negotiate and, if possible, be prepared to compromise.
- Find opportunities to show you trust your adolescent. If you are disappointed, try again.

- Encourage your adolescent to become involved in fun and challenging activities so that they can experience success and feel positive about life. Keep them busy! Show your interest and praise achievements. Ignore the negatives you can live with.
- Make sure that your adolescent feels connected – loved, valued and, above all, listened to.
- Take time out for yourself. You need to look after your sanity and replenish your energy. It's often easier to see things in perspective with a little distance and renewed strength. It's also important for children to respect this need for parents to have time out.
- Have someone to talk to for the times when you will need support. Being able to talk things over and have a laugh with a friend or another parent of adolescents can help enormously. You'll usually discover that you aren't coping too badly after all. The support of family members and close friends can be invaluable. Knowing that there are others closely involved in their adolescent's life can give parents great relief. Grandparents are often the most precious avenues of help, but good friends are also important. In addition to acting as 'sounding boards' for parents, they can also sometimes become the all-important 'significant other' so greatly needed by young people.

Friendship and laughter

To be a parent of teenagers you need a good friend and a sense of humour. The friend is to reassure you that you are not alone and you will survive. The sense of humour is to be able to laugh at yourself and the ridiculous mess you sometimes get into in your relationship with your children. In the middle of a discussion with my fourteen-year-old daughter, she told me that I don't understand where she is coming from because she has middle child syndrome. I replied, 'Well actually, darling, I do understand. I too suffered middle child syndrome.' She went on to tell me that was different because I was the middle of six children whereas she is truly the middle of three. At that point we both realised the ridiculous nature of our conversation and laughed at ourselves.

As parents of toddlers, we put incredible energy into encouraging our children to be independent and we rejoice in their attempts to do things on their own. Ten years later, when they want to exercise that independence, we freak out. I need to constantly remind myself that independent people making decisions for themselves is what I desire for my children. One of my daughters says a good parent is one who trusts their child's judgement.

As a parent of teenagers, you also need to continually remind yourself that you love them – it's the behaviour that you don't like. My children need to be frequently told that I love them regardless of their behaviour. I make sure I tell each of them once a day. It's a good reminder for all of us.

Ruth Wallbridge

Many hands make lighter work

I am married, the mother of two children and a general practitioner. I commenced having a family in my thirties. I felt nervous about having children, having been the first child of my parents who each divorced and remarried several times. I was also nervous about combining motherhood with my professional career. Nevertheless, I did want to have children, regarding it as one of life's special experiences.

From the early days of both our daughters' lives, a number of our extended family members and friends bonded with each infant and formed links, that have endured. The rich texture of these numerous relationships has offered our daughters much more than we, as their parents alone, could have provided.

 Nan Presswell, mother of Natasha and Tania

CRUNCH TIME

The hair! The clothes!

What is the best response if your adolescent comes home sporting black from head to toe, with the exception of green tips in the Gothic black hair?

☐ Be totally honest. Laugh
☐ Order them to grow up, act their age and take the ridiculous outfit off
☐ Stay calm. Ask them how the day has been
☐ Ask what time the carnival begins

Be totally honest. Laugh

If you do, this might be the last laugh you have for a while. And don't forget to duck for cover! Adolescents are super sensitive about their appearance and it's best to avoid criticisms. This is not a good time to be brutally honest if you want to get through the next few years with your sanity intact.

Order them to grow up, act their age and take the ridiculous outfit off

Once again, dangerous words! They will only hurt, infuriate and alienate your adolescent. And, after all, they are actually trying to grow up. The outfits, head gear and other miscellaneous adornments are simply part of that searching for the 'real me' all adolescents go through as they try to 'grow up'. Hang in there and keep all opinions about the 'searching-for-self' costumes well hidden. If necessary, invest in strong hair gel to prevent your eyebrows from raising of their own accord each time you sight your beloved offspring. Take heart! Most young people do eventually emerge from this colourful stage looking surprisingly normal.

Stay calm. Ask them how the day has been

Yes! You'll eventually get better and better at controlling the blood pressure. Avoid mentioning the things that are not life threatening and focus on the positives. The important element is the happiness of your adolescent and the happiness of the whole family. Negative or sarcastic comments will only cause anger and unhappiness for everyone. Overlook behaviour that isn't worth fighting over. Save your strength for those days when you'll really need it.

Ask what time the carnival begins

Likely to produce a range of rather unpleasant reactions from your adolescent. Keep in mind that adolescents are often more gifted in the use of sarcasm than the most mentally agile adult.

Middle adolescence at a glance

This is a time of:

- Emancipation from parents
- Focus shifting dramatically from family to peers
- Identifying with particular forms of music, youth icons etc.
- Seeking individuality by spurning adult control and support
- Possibly strained relationships with parents
- Needing a 'guide' who can help nourish adolescents' uniqueness

4

Late adolescence — 'What is my place in the world?'

This is a great opportunity for parents to really show their interest in the plans and decisions adolescents need to make.

Late adolescents are struggling to find their place in the world. This is the stage of the journey when young people begin to mature and to fully face up to all that has been happening. They have to *confront their identity crisis* and they have to actually answer that question, *'Who am I?'*, which they began grappling with in middle adolescence. One or two generations ago, late adolescents would often be in full-time employment and be moving out of the family home. In today's world, however, many young people at this stage are facing a more uncertain world as far as studies and employment are concerned. This naturally increases stress on young people, and parents need to be sensitive to this. Many employment opportunities are not open to young people unless they continue to study for a few years after the completion of secondary education. Consequently, many late adolescents continue to live at home rather than move out on their own. While these changes are not inherently bad in themselves, they do mean that adolescents either consciously or unconsciously seek other ways to mark their separation from their parents.

> A child becomes an adult when he realises that he has a right not only to be right but also to be wrong.
>
> **Thomas Szasz**

Give your unconditional support

Late adolescents are seeking to define and understand their functional role in life. To find their place in the world. Often, this is the time when they begin to *value* their parents once again. In making important decisions about directions for the future, young people need support from parents. This is a great opportunity for parents to

really show their interest in plans and decisions adolescents need to make. This is a particularly difficult time for adolescents, with an increasing emphasis being placed on academic success.

Parents need to reassure adolescents that parental love and support are not conditional upon glowing results. Adolescents who do not achieve the highest scores in the final years of secondary education need to know their value as a person is in no way diminished; their future success in no way diminished.

Make it clear

Every time we drive past University X, Dad smiles and says, 'That's where you're going, Amanda.' When he says this I feel like I can't live up to his expectations. I don't think I can get the marks. It's pressure. He's not a bad person or anything ... he's a good dad. He just doesn't know how hard it is for me to hear that all the time. Sometimes, when I'm alone, it makes me cry.

Amanda, 16

Considering another road

When one of my sons had finished his second last year at secondary school, and it was obvious that his enthusiasm for school had waned considerably, he came to me and said he didn't want to go on to studies the next year. His school agreed that a year off wouldn't be a bad idea. My son said he wanted to go to France for a year and displayed great initiative in getting information about various cultural exchange programs. Off he went. On his return he spoke fluent French, had a very expensive taste in wine and more life experience under his belt. He had also acquired a completely different attitude to academic work.

Not all young people will necessarily be ready to do the final years of school when school and parents say so. Parents need to be flexible and ready to consider other options.

Michael

Into the unknown

Whether young people choose to continue post-secondary studies or to go into the workforce, this is a time of great change for them. They are faced with some huge questions:

- What is the right course and career for me?
- What will I do if I have made the wrong choice?
- What does the world outside hold for me?
- Will I be able to make new friends at university and work?
- Will I be able to cope with the new demands?
- What will Mum and Dad say if I don't make a success of things?
- How will Mum and Dad react if I tell them that I don't want to study any more?

Being there when it counts

As a careers counsellor, I assist young people going on to further education or employment. As each of these young people leaves my office, I always stand up and reach out to shake hands with an often surprised student. 'I'm so happy for you. I really think you'll enjoy this course. I'd love to hear all about what you are doing, so keep in touch. Good on you!' Young people are often surprised when I shake their hands. The surprise, however, is almost always replaced by such a glow of pleasure that, at times, I have been almost moved to tears – especially when the young person before me is visibly moved. What are they thinking? Probably a mixture of emotions. Apprehension about the unknown future, sometimes sadness at leaving school and maybe just happiness that someone believes in them.

This handshaking has really taken off! A large group of students saw me shake hands with a student outside my office. They came in to discuss what to do after receiving their results, and one of them beat me to the gun. As he stood up to leave, he reached out and firmly shook my hand. Few things render me speechless, but for a split second I was silenced. How gorgeous, I was thinking. Young people need to feel that they are seen as important people by the adults in their lives and that these adults would be proud to shake hands with them. I did a lot of handshaking that day.

If a simple handshake from a careers counsellor can mean so much to young people, imagine how much more a similar gesture would mean coming from parents, grandparents, brothers and sisters! A handshake encapsulates so much. It shows that you are meeting a young person on an equal footing, that there has been a shift in the relationship. You are giving a tangible sign that you believe they are growing up, becoming an adult, moving on to important and exciting things. But, most of all, it's a sign that you respect that young person. Such a simple, yet enormously important gesture. Of course, there are other great ways parents can demonstrate pride in their children; an arm around the shoulder, a spontaneous hug or a pat on the back. At those important milestones in a young person's life, these gestures all say, 'I'm proud of you. I have faith in you.' While you're at it, tell them you are proud of them. Say it out loud. And, I can't recommend the handshake or other physical gestures of respect too highly! Young people love them.

Erin

Young people are often quite frightened during this period of great change. As a society, we place so much emphasis on the move from secondary school to higher education or to work. Young people moving out into the unknown need to know that parents and the family are a source of constant support and stability. Parents and the family are a safe haven to which a young person can return at any time. Make sure your children know you will not 'hit the roof' if things go wrong at the new job or in the new course of study.

While some young people will handle this period of change with little effort, others will struggle. Parents need to look out for signs that a young person may be feeling 'lost' at this time and be ready to show understanding and support.

Car, dog or holiday? Parental incentives to study

I have encountered some incredible parental 'incentives' to 'encourage' adolescents to study hard. One student was offered a car if she gained entry to a prestigious university, and a dog if she only managed average results. Another student was told that if she gained a certain level of results, the entire family would be going on a great holiday – if not, they would all be staying home. (An effective way to encourage sibling rivalry – the brothers and sisters monitored every move this young person made!) Yet another student was not allowed to watch any television for the entire final year of school, was to receive no incoming phone calls and to make no calls, and was not allowed to contact any of his friends. All of these students feared their parents and, sadly, while they were also resentful of what was happening to them, they still desperately craved the approval and acceptance of the parents. It's very difficult to support these young people when they feel so detached from their parents and afraid of letting them down.

What happened to them? The first student got the dog and loves it but she is still dealing with the perception that she has disappointed her parents. The second student and her family did go on that holiday, but I witnessed a very burnt-out and insecure young person go off, looking more like she had lost than won. The third student didn't do as well as his parents expected (all work and no play?), and went off the rails at university, perhaps dealing with internalised anger.

Without doubt, the happiest young people I see are those who are given the clear message that they are more important than any academic result. They are then free to focus on study, knowing they are not fighting to maintain parental love and approval. They already have these.

Erin

Respect your adolescent's decisions

Respecting decisions made by an adolescent at this important stage is a great way to demonstrate that you regard them as a young adult. This is a time when the relationship with an adolescent must be based upon mutual respect and affection. For a young person to actually become a young adult, they must be given the opportunity to make important decisions and to feel that parents will respect those decisions. You can offer invaluable support by becoming involved in career planning and applications for jobs. Offer to drive your adolescent to an interview, or meet for coffee afterwards. Young people need to be supported, especially during times when they are unsuccessful in obtaining entry to a particular course or obtaining a certain job.

Say it out loud

Adolescents can't read minds. Parents should verbalise their feelings of pride in their adolescents because many young people actually need to hear the words to know that they are valued. Parents need to ensure that young people at this crucial stage of life feel that their achievements are recognised and valued. At significant times such as graduation from secondary school or acceptance into a tertiary course or apprenticeship, the family needs to

celebrate together. These are unique opportunities for the family to come together and to affirm the worth of a young person. The actual level of academic results should not determine the level of celebration.

Put it all into perspective

Parents can reassure young people that, in choosing post-secondary courses or a job, they don't have to 'get it right' the first time. Young people need to hear that it is okay to test the waters and change direction. They should not feel that they have failed or wasted time if their first course of study or job does not fulfil expectations. This is a perfect opportunity for parents to teach young people that every experience is valuable and that what is important is to continue to search for that dream course or career.

Show pride

Young people are quick to recognise if parents are disappointed in them. The overriding message from parents should be, 'We are proud of you and we love you.' This is not the time to blame or accuse a young person for not studying hard enough. Most young people are all too quick to blame themselves. They need to learn to accept a less than desired result, to make the best of it and to *move forward* with renewed energy. This is a huge task for adolescents, even with the full support of parents. The media will ensure that images of the 'most successful' students are in full view. Parents need to ensure that all of this is put into perspective. Nothing is more important than a young person feeling 'connected' to the family and knowing that they will always have the support of parents. This will help a young person handle academic or personal disap-pointments at this stage and to move on with life.

Notice warning signs

Parents need to watch for warning signs that a young person is not adjusting well to the changes during late adolescence. Sometimes young people initially feel overwhelmed in huge and new environments such as those at university and in the workforce. Many will lose contact with school friends who have offered great support in the past. Many believe that they will disappoint parents if they don't 'measure up' and consequently have a constant fear of failing. Parents need to be alert for signs of stress and make time to talk things through. Some young people may even be misreading messages from parents. It is important to make sure that parental thoughts about the whole area of careers and courses is clear. Warning signs that things are not going well for late adolescents can be:

- Moodiness, changes in behaviour, loss of interest in life, generally looking unhappy
- Reluctance to talk about studies or career
- Loss of contact with 'old' friends and no new friendships being established
- Inability to sleep
- Changes in eating patterns
- Withdrawal from family activities
- Sudden and uncharacteristic changes in behaviour – destructive, dangerous and reckless behaviour and high risk taking

Celebrate the milestones

Apart from the move to further education or to employment, late adolescence is a time full of important milestones for young people. They reach the age where they can vote for the first time, obtain a car licence and legally gain entry to adult venues. It's also often the time when the first serious relationships are forming. Parents should try to celebrate each of these events and show real pride in their adolescents as they reach these milestones. Parents can, for example, be involved in teaching their adolescents to drive, and can offer support and encouragement in all other areas. Parents can greatly strengthen the relationship with their adolescents by actively demonstrating their respect for this new young adult. Late adolescents are often very vulnerable and afraid of the many changes they are facing. The support of parents is invaluable. It can make the transition from late adolescence to adulthood a smoother and happier time for a young person and, indeed, the entire family. We all remember our first rejections, our first success in landing a job, our first serious love. Be there for your children when they need you most.

Survival hints for late adolescence

- Talk things through. This is a challenging time, when new experiences are being met daily. Young people need to hear that it is normal to need some time to adjust to a new course of study or a new career. Moving out of the relatively 'safe' secondary school environment to post-secondary studies or work is a huge transition.
- Encourage new interests. Encourage young people to join clubs and participate in activities where new friendships can be formed. At the time of transition from secondary school to higher education or to work, many young people lose contact with former friends. Re-establishing a new support group is very important.
- Maintain family cohesion. Young people who have begun a new phase in their lives, such as work or higher education, still need

parental support. Some hide their insecurity behind a veneer of bravado, afraid to admit that they are confused or worried when they often need the reassurance of parents more than ever. A good 'ice breaker' is for parents to share their own experiences of beginning work or higher education with their adolescent. Adolescents need to see that their parents are interested in what they are doing and that they understand it is a challenging time.

Most young people in late adolescence do finally emerge from the **hormonal fog** that has engulfed them since puberty hit and they again see things with clarity and realise that their parents aren't so bad after all. Yes, the wonderful child you once knew is back and, most importantly, is *human again*. Take heart. No matter how tough the going sometimes gets, most adolescents survive their own adolescence!

Thankfully, most adolescents at this stage do again begin to view their parents as a support rather than as adversaries. This is a great relief for parents who are, understandably, often quite frazzled after such a roller coaster ride. Some cynics may put this change in adolescents down to the fact that they have finally figured out they do need the food, the car, money, clothes and shelter that parents provide. Whatever the reason, the relief parents feel can be almost tangible.

Appreciating home

It's been Jessie, my elder sister Katie and myself since I was eight months old. We left my dad in Cairns and moved to Brisbane to be with my grandmother. Growing up, I knew we were in a different situation from most families. Mum was the sole breadwinner and worked hard at a job she was good at. But she also made sure the job was five houses down from the primary school my sister and I attended so she was near in case of an emergency. The quality I most admire in Mum has been her self-sacrifice. She is always ready to put herself out for the demands of an eighteen-year-old daughter (namely 4 a.m. phone calls asking to be picked up) and does it without the grumpiness you would expect from most parents.

Mum is unorthodox. She always believed in letting us think for ourselves and discovering the repercussions of our sometimes bad decisions. But her *advice is wise. Mum has raised me to be an individual, capable of realising the truths of the world over a cup of tea on her bed with her. She is someone I aspire to be like. She's an original, that's for sure …*

Alexandra Gooderham, 18

Adolescents who can safely voice opinions without fear of rejection and who are shown real trust, have a great start in their young adult lives. They know where they belong and it's a good place to be.

CRUNCH TIME

Conflict!

How should you respond if your adolescent threatens to leave home?

- ☐ Offer to help pack their bags
- ☐ Ignore the comment
- ☐ Dig deeply to find the reasons why this comment is being made
- ☐ Say you can't wait to see the back of them

Offer to help pack their bags

Tempting! Very tempting! But probably not a good way to go unless you do want them to leave. Your flippant response is likely to anger your adolescent to the point where they won't want to back down. Of course, you may simply be trying to lighten the atmosphere with a little humour and all your good intentions backfire. Only you can judge whether your adolescent is in the mood for a light-hearted response or not. Survey the scene carefully before making a comment like this.

Ignore the comment

Not a bad way to go. Much better than exploding or using sarcasm. Be careful though. Some young people actually do run away from home. They mean it. And most parents don't really want their kids to disappear – not until they are ready, anyway. Remember how sensitive adolescents are: nitroglycerin is more stable than the temperament of most! Many young people present a tough 'I don't care attitude' when, in fact, they are very fragile. They are easily hurt and hurt often turns to anger.

Dig deeply to find the reasons why this comment is being made

... Yes! What's going wrong? Is it university or work? Parents? Siblings? Can things be changed so that everyone is better off? Establishing positive communication with your adolescent is one of the very best ways to make sure they are happy and less likely to go 'off the rails'. If young people believe that their opinion really counts and that they are able to voice their concerns without fearing rejection or ridicule, you're halfway there!

Say you can't wait to see the back of them

If you're lucky, you'll have only verbal abuse thrown back at you. If not, perhaps some of the furniture close by. If your luck is running low, you might be searching for a recent photo to send to the Missing Persons file. Insults and adolescents don't make for a happy outcome.

summary

Late adolescence at a glance

This is a time of:

- Facing up to and confronting the identity crisis
- Seeking to define and understand the functional role in life
- Relationships based on mutual respect and affection
- Increased display of commitment and responsibility
- Planning for the future
- Needing assistance in setting clear objectives and planning strategies to achieve goals
- Realising that parents aren't so bad after all

CHAPTER 5

The tasks of adolescence

The four tasks are achieved
during early, middle and late
adolescence, and often there is
no clear beginning or end of
each task.

To lead a psychologically, emotionally and physically healthy life, adolescents have to successfully achieve *four tasks* during adolescence. The successful achievement of each task signals that an adolescent is moving closer to becoming an independent adult.

> When I was a boy of fourteen, my father was so ignorant I could hardly stand to have the old man around. But when I got to be twenty-one, I was astonished at how much the old man had learned in seven years.
>
> **Mark Twain**

The four tasks of adolescence

1. To form a secure and positive identity
2. To achieve independence from adult carers and parents
3. To establish love objects outside the family
4. To find a place in the world by establishing career direction and economic independence

These four tasks are achieved during early, middle and late adolescence, and often there is no clear beginning or end of each task. Young people begin to achieve some tasks in early adolescence and won't fully confront them until late adolescence. Other tasks usually begin in middle adolescence and are 'completed' in late adolescence.

Some of the tasks are questions we all face and continually redefine over our lives. A question like 'Who am I?' can be asked many times. An understanding of these developmental tasks is fundamental to an understanding of some of the behaviour of adolescents.

Today, young people are trying to 'find themselves' in a world that is changing at an increasingly bewildering pace. They are facing a future that is in many ways more uncertain environmentally, politically, economically, vocationally and spiritually than at any other time in recorded history. Events such as the destruction of the World Trade Centre in New York, and other acts of terrorism, have jolted the entire world. These are just one indication of what could lead young people to interpret the world as a frightening and unpredictable place to grow up in. Remember, it is against this constantly changing background that adolescents must achieve the four tasks of adolescence.

1. To form a secure and positive identity

This task begins in early adolescence and continues right through to late adolescence. What happens in childhood sets the scene for this first task to be either easy, difficult or extremely difficult. Young people who approach adolescence with a positive self-esteem and a clear knowledge that they are safe and loved are better able to achieve this task.

Forming a secure and positive identity is probably *the ultimate goal of adolescence.* The achievement of a positive sense of self has an effect upon a young person's ability to form relationships and successfully negotiate other tasks of adolescence. In other words, young people have to *figure out who they are*. This is no easy task. It involves an adolescent asking huge questions and making decisions about issues, values, beliefs and ethics. In essence it involves arriving at a point of self-understanding and self-acceptance.

This scrutiny of oneself can be exhausting and even frightening if an adolescent comes to believe that they are unacceptable in the eyes of others. *Adolescents who feel worthless or unacceptable are prevented from forming a positive identity*. Some begin to hide their true feelings and to play a role they believe will be acceptable. Some are also afraid to admit certain feelings they have or to accept particular aspects of themselves, and they stagnate emotionally. Others are unable to sort out *who* they are and *what* they want to be. These young people are experiencing *identity confusion*. They are understandably frightened and can become moody, angry and depressed, feeling as if they are in a huge black hole from which they cannot escape.

How parents can help

- Give your adolescent lots of affirmation. Find opportunities to praise achievements, skills and character attributes. It is just as fantastic to have a son or daughter who is thoughtful and generous as one who is good at algebra. Parents can help young people build a positive self-image by recognising their strengths and commenting on these.

- If parents begin to realise that their adolescent has low self-esteem, it's important to address this by giving the young person lots of affirmation. In a practical sense, it is also important to help the young person identify possible new interests and areas of strength. This may involve encouraging the young person to take up a new hobby so that self-esteem can be strengthened.

- Parents must make certain adolescents feels valued and accepted, warts and all. Loved unconditionally! It is important to give the message that a young person's worth is *not* measured by academic success, sporting ability or high achievement in any particular field, but by their willingness to give life a go. This message, if conveyed wholeheartedly by parents, can give young people a wonderful sense of freedom. The pressure is off! Young people who are not pressured to achieve a high level of success, are not afraid to try. The stakes are not terrifying. Parental acceptance, approval and love are not being risked.

- Parents can ensure that their adolescent has a clear understanding that they are loved regardless of whether they are academically brilliant, average or struggling at school; wishing to pursue a traditional or non-traditional career; heterosexual, bisexual or homosexual; outgoing or reserved; prefers sport or the arts.

- The message young people need to hear from parents is, *'You are loved and nothing can change that.'* This will give adolescents a much-needed feeling of security and belonging. They will feel connected rather than fearing that any moment they disappoint parents they will be disconnected.

- Young people who feel accepted and able to be themselves find the task of forming a positive identity much easier than a young person who is afraid of rejection and who has low self-esteem.

- Adolescents will find the task of identity formation much easier if, as young children, they have been given the freedom to be themselves. Parents can help enormously by encouraging their children to pursue interests and actively praising them for their achievements. Children who have developed a positive sense of self and are aware that their parents are proud of their skills and talents, will have a head start on the road to self-acceptance and ultimately the formation of a positive identity.

Know your child

We have two sons. Mark is seven and James is three. When Mark was born, I thought, Right, he's going to be a doctor. I thought it would be a great helping profession. Then, when I saw that his talents were in another area, I eventually let go of the doctor idea. It's not fair to project your desires on to another person. I might make other mistakes, but I won't make this one. I also wanted Mark to love reading and writing like me. My intuition soon told me that he's not going to be that. He's mechanical. I've got to love him for who he is. I've realised that you can't mould your children into what you might want. You can only offer them as many different things as you can, and just foster what they are interested in.

Our family doctor was the first person to notice that Mark has a mind with a mechanical bent. He always asks questions about how things work. Then he started to draw things like circuit boards. He's taken our broken video player apart and puts pieces of it together. We've seen a very hyperactive kid at his happiest when he's playing with electronics. I once said to him, 'Wind down. You're overexcited. What would help you feel better?' He replied, 'Mum, I actually relax when I'm doing my electronics projects.' My husband Geoff and I can't help him with all of this. Geoff's artistic and I'm just learning what a 'capacitor' is. It's something electronic. So we buy Mark simple electronic kits and his uncle comes over and they put them together. He's even got a *Make it Yourself* electronics book. He can't read it all but he loves the pictures.

Already I can see that James is very different from Mark. Mark is not particularly interested in a story but James loves books and will sit for hours looking at them. He's more like me in this respect. Sometimes I go crazy though because he wants the same story read over and over again. James is also more emotionally intuitive than Mark. If he sees me upset, he says, 'Mummy, don't worry. It's okay.' Mark's not musical but James loves music. Mark has to take things apart. James admires their beauty. He doesn't care how they work.

I love books and Geoff loves art. Mark might not be an artist or a writer or a doctor. Then again, he may. That's fine. He's happy. James is engrossed in his books. He's happy. Watching our children grow, we've come to realise that what is important is to develop and support their interests, not ours. We hope they will further develop those interests as they approach adolescence.

 Sarah

2. To achieve independence from adult carers and parents

This breaking away from parents begins in early adolescence, continues through middle adolescence and into late adolescence. The achievement of this task can create some conflict between parents and young people.

Parents are in the unenviable position of having to adjust to being questioned, criticised, ignored and perhaps even disobeyed. Teachers too! Young people do, however, have to achieve emotional independence from adults in order to continue the process of becoming young adults themselves. This means making *friends* outside the family, friends who are needed and necessary supports.

How parents can help

- In order to feel a sense of independence from parents, adolescents need to be given *the opportunity to experience independence* and consequently to learn *how to handle independence*. Parents should *not be too overprotective* at this time as this will almost certainly

provoke anger from an adolescent and prevent them learning how to handle independence and make more adult decisions.

- As adults, we have **to trust adolescents enough to loosen the ties** and to allow them to demonstrate independent thought and action. If young people are allowed to taste independence in small doses, and are then rewarded with genuine praise, they will learn how to accept responsibility. They will also learn to appreciate the good feeling of being trusted.

- A great way to allow young people to experience a sense of independence is to make them responsible for a particular task around home. An even greater sense of achievement and independence for young people comes with landing that first 'real' job. This can be a daunting experience for adolescents. Parents can help young people find part-time work by looking for opportunities and helping out with suggestions on how to approach prospective employers: what to wear, say and not to say. Having a job is a fantastic boost to self-esteem and also allows adolescents to expand their circle of friends and to generally feel good about life. It's also an opportunity for the whole family to celebrate this new achievement or milestone in a young person's life.

- Another way to encourage a young person to taste independence is to gradually teach them to be responsible about money and budgeting. Small amounts of pocket money can be increased to an 'allowance' for older adolescents. Learning how to spend this wisely, to make it last or to save for a special purchase are all valuable lessons.
- At some point your adolescent will disappoint you. This is when it is important to forgive and to move on, and to trust again, and again. Being overprotective may actually prevent your adolescent from growing up and developing independent adult thoughts and action. Young people crave the opportunity to show they can be trusted. Parents need to provide opportunities for adolescents to demonstrate they can be trusted.
- Don't feel threatened or abandoned if your adolescent suddenly begins and ends each sentence with a quote from their newly acquired mentor or friends. This is simply another part of the breaking away from parents. It's a natural and healthy part of growing up. Your adolescent probably still listens to what you say, although often making a great effort to appear to disregard every word you utter. It is important to present your thoughts in a calm manner while allowing your young person to feel that their opinion counts, too. Adolescents do not like to feel that adults have already made up their minds and that expressing an opinion is simply exercising vocal cords. The most common reaction from adolescents who feel this way is to attack parents with quite a virulent outpouring of abuse, followed by a glass-shattering slamming of any door between the adolescent and the front gate.
- Providing opportunities for young people to show independence, and respecting their opinions and feelings, will most certainly assist you to gain their attention and respect.

3. To establish love objects outside the family

This task cuts across early, middle and late adolescence, becoming more important for young people at each stage. Establishing 'love objects' outside the family can be seen as beginning in a sense with the high importance placed upon friends in early adolescence. The importance of the peer group cannot be overestimated. Young people place an incredibly high value on the acceptance of their friends. A break-up of a friendship can be very distressing for a young person, and parents do need to be sensitive to this.

In middle adolescence, friends assume an even greater importance, and adolescents desperately want to go out in friendship groups. This is closely followed by young people beginning to pair off with a girlfriend or boyfriend, sometimes in middle adolescence and then more seriously in late adolescence. Late adolescents are, in effect, searching for a soulmate. These relationships anchor them in the journey away from adults and parents, and are an important milestone for young people.

This can be a very trying time for parents who don't 'approve' of the chosen love object. Broaching this subject with a young person requires the dexterity of a snake handler! Try to remember how all-consuming that first love can be. Even friendships consume the attention and energy of young children and adolescents. They are devastated if they are ignored by a friend, heartbroken if a fight occurs. For an adolescent, the break-up of a relationship is felt as a real loss, and parents need to appreciate that a young person may need extra care around this time.

TANDBERG

The importance of friends

> I was counselling a seventeen-year-old girl who was terminally ill with cancer. This girl had been in hospital for a while and she had begun to get abusive towards her parents, nurses and other care givers. I was asked to come and see her. When I visited, I noticed that her parents had literally set up camp in her room. For 24 hours of the day, one of her parents or the other was in this small, cramped room. When I arrived, I had to ask them to leave so I could talk privately with my patient. They reluctantly left. Very quickly it emerged that her parents were driving her nuts. While she loved them, and appreciated the care and attention they were giving her, she wanted to see her friends who felt they couldn't intrude on the family. Despite the fact that this girl was dying, she was still a young person and still wanted to be with her friends. A tactful and respectful discussion with parents took place and a few close friends began to visit. The girl died a few weeks later with family and close friends in the room.
>
> **Michael**

How parents can help

- Communicate any real concerns you may have about a chosen partner with great sensitivity. A helpful way to begin such a discussion is to stress how much your adolescent is valued by the family and that you are simply concerned for their welfare.
- Unless the chosen love object is seen as presenting a genuine risk to an adolescent's wellbeing, parents should generally refrain from commenting. A friend with clothes and hair that glow in the dark should not prompt a serious family discussion. Parents should initiate a discussion with their adolescent, however, if the 'friend' is obviously violent, appears to be involved in illicit drugs or other high risk-taking behaviours. Even in this case, parents should approach the discussion carefully and be sensitive to the feelings of their adolescent. Presenting concerns in the context of being a loving parent who doesn't want their young person to be hurt by

their friends is a good beginning. This is a positive message for a young person to hear and won't alienate them, as will the comment, 'How could you be friends with a loser like that?' or 'You aren't allowed to mix with people like that.'

- Listening to a young person's opinion is extremely important. Sometimes, being able to talk about the love object in a non-threatening and nonjudgemental way may actually result in a young person seeing their friend in a new light. Young people simply don't want to be lectured or to be told that their girlfriend or boyfriend is 'no good'. They want to feel that their opinions and choices are respected.
- The establishment of a love object is extremely important for adolescents, and consequently, the break-up of a relationship can be a very difficult time for these young people. It's not a good idea for parents to show they are actually happy that a relationship has broken up. This reaction can generate anger, hurt and resentment.
- Parents can help greatly by showing their understanding and concern. Some young people may not want to talk about the details of what has happened, but just knowing that parents are concerned can provide great security and comfort for them. Others will

welcome the opportunity to talk. After a relationship break-up, most young people don't want to hear, 'There are plenty of fish in the sea'. Although well intentioned, a comment like this can have the effect of making a young person feel that parents don't understand. Young people need to know that parents do care and are ready to listen if and when the young person wants to talk.

4. To find a place in the world by establishing career direction and economic independence

This begins to some extent in middle adolescence, but becomes very important in late adolescence. In middle adolescence, many young people begin to think about career direction. In late adolescence, they are required to consider long-term plans and goals.

If adolescents are lucky, somewhere along the adolescent journey, they will meet a person who will inspire them, hear an inspirational speech, see a film or read a book, and they'll begin to think, Yeah, that's what I want to be. That's what I really want to do with my life! Some adolescents don't stumble upon such a revelation and will need help from parents in investigating possible career options.

Young people today face a competitive market to enter employment or tertiary studies. It is important, however, to help young people put this into perspective. Many adolescents begin to worry about unemployment from an increasingly younger age. The message for young people today is to obtain those high scores or they're 'stuffed'. These 'messages' are greatly exaggerated and misleading for young people during a fragile time in their lives. Such negativity often crushes the very idealism and exuberance that can be such a wonderful aspect of youth.

Vocational decisions often cause unnecessary anxiety for both adolescents and parents, and some simple steps can prevent a lot of heartache and slammed doors. A more realistic look at the whole business of course and career choice, scores and employment is fundamental for parents to be able to support their adolescent. What is the truth behind those negative messages young people are often receiving? What can parents do to ease the pressures?

How parents can help

- Many adolescents see career choice as an overwhelming task. If the relationship with an adolescent has become strained, this is a wonderful opportunity for parents to 'be there' for their adolescent. A sensitive approach can strengthen bonds that may have weakened. This is a time when well-informed and supportive parents can make a world of difference to young people. Choosing a course of study and a vocational direction is an extremely important step, and adolescents need to feel that they have the encouragement and involvement of the people who matter the most – the family.

- When the time arrives for narrowing down the choice of subjects to study, encourage your adolescent to select subjects they enjoy and are good at. It's a real concern when young people say that Mum or Dad insist they study a particular stream of maths, or physics or any other subject for that matter. *It is important for young people to feel that they have some choice in what they are studying*. It is difficult for a young person to do well in a subject they do not enjoy. An adolescent who loves art should be allowed to study art. An adolescent who loves chemistry should study chemistry. Encourage young people to pursue areas they are passionate about.

- High marks are great but they are not so important that young people should spend months living in fear and sleepless nights dreading a lower than 'acceptable' score. High marks are not as important as the health and happiness of your adolescent. Many young people talk about the terror they live in at the thought of having to face parents and friends and neighbours if that score isn't 'good enough'. In the mind of a young person, this translates as, 'I am not good enough. I'm a failure. I've let everyone down!'. Reassure your adolescent that your love won't be changed because of school results. The message your adolescent needs to hear is, 'You are not your final score! One score does not have the power to destroy the entire future!' Regardless of the reason why your young person may not have achieved the highest scores, they need to feel valued and loved.

- If your adolescent didn't work as hard as possible, or partied too hard, this isn't the time to let loose with the lecture. It's a difficult enough time already, and a better approach is to encourage a young person to move on. Young people all mature at different times and some simply aren't ready for the disciplined approach to studies needed in the final years of secondary education. Many young people blossom at a later stage.

- Demonstrate your trust and belief in your adolescent by allowing *them* to make that final decision about subjects and careers. This is a great way to show that you do see your adolescent as a young adult capable of making decisions. If the pressure from parents is too great, some adolescents simply choose what their parents want. This will prevent a young person from growing up and making adult decisions, and from successfully achieving one of the important tasks of adolescence – the achievement of a vocational identity.

- Academic institutions offer courses that can be a stepping stone to university studies at a later date. Adolescents in their final year of secondary education should be aware of all pathways to their chosen career area or interest area. If young people can see that everything does not hinge upon gaining entry to one course alone, then the *stress level* many are experiencing will be greatly reduced.

- Talk to your adolescent about the big picture. It's important that young people know that adults don't measure their worth as a person by academic success. Does your adolescent know this is how you feel? Do they know that what is most important to you is their happiness? It's important to express these thoughts because many young people assume that their parents will see them differently, love them less if academic results are lower than expected. Parents can help enormously by finding stories of role models who have achieved their goals in inspirational ways. Give your adolescent the clear message that it's not all about academic success.

School results

My dad was sitting beside me as I accessed my final results. He had been telling me for so long not to be disappointed if I didn't do as well as I wanted. He was very happy about my score. He kept ringing me from work that day. My mum kept on hugging me and saying, 'Wow!'

 Katherine, 19

I felt disappointed with the score I received partly due to the fact that my parents were disappointed with it. Dad would not talk to me. He even left the house to get away from me. He didn't say anything. I just sat there ... Mum was okay ...

Jason, 17

My family are very important to me. I know that whatever I choose to do or who I become as a person, my family will always be behind me. Whatever dreams I follow or goals I achieve, I will owe a lot of it to my parents who have taught me all about unconditional love. They show me this not just in the things they say, but in what they do. I hope one day I will be able to show my children these things.

Lauren Traugott, 18

Investigating careers can be exciting

The exciting aspect of my work as a careers counsellor is to see the eyes of students light up when they discover the course or career of their dreams. The heartbreaking part of my work, though, is trying to offer support and comfort to those students whose parents have unrealistically high expectations of them. Some parents also refuse to listen to what their children actually want to do as far as courses and careers go. These students are extremely unhappy and aren't looking to the future with excitement. I often find myself telling students and parents about my own family in an attempt to restore some sanity to the picture. I tell them that my two brothers both disliked school and did not immediately go on to higher education. I am pleased to add that both, later on when they were ready, completed extensive studies: Michael went on to run a hospitality business and then to become a pilot, and Jerome became first a hotel manager, then a builder, and then moved on to run a catering business and a farm. Students love to hear stories like this.

Growing up, my brothers and I were lucky to have parents who simply wanted us to be happy and encouraged us to do what we wanted to do. Recently, when we lost my brother Jerome in a tragic accident, I was comforted with the thought that he had lived his life to the full and always had my parents' support when he decided to change career direction — over and over! I often tell parents of my students about my brothers. I hope that they will give their adolescents the freedom to follow their hearts and to feel the unconditional support that my brothers and I were fortunate to have from our parents.

Erin

CRUNCH TIME

Careers

What is the most appropriate response to make if your adolescent announces he wants to be a hairdresser?

- ☐ 'You're joking! That's not a proper job for a man! You don't want people to say you're a sissy, do you?'
- ☐ 'That's new. When did you decide this? Let's hear all about it.'
- ☐ 'Okay. Whatever.'
- ☐ 'But you're doing so well at school. Why throw it all away? You can do better than that!'
- ☐ 'Great! Free haircuts!'

'You're joking! That's not a proper job for a man! You don't want people to say you're a sissy, do you?'

Searching for a possible direction in life can be a stressful time for your adolescent. Ruling out certain career areas can place young people in a very difficult position. By limiting choices you risk limiting your child's happiness. As long as your adolescent is a happy, confident young person, does it really matter if he is a hairdresser?

'That's new. When did you decide this? Let's hear all about it.'

Yes! It's great to show genuine interest in your adolescent's life and choices and to show your willingness to really listen. By doing this, you'll be providing the kind of support that will make your adolescent feel heard, understood and valued. He will also be less likely to go out and do something capable of turning your hair grey overnight! Sometimes the latest career choice of an adolescent may come out of left field. Rather than reacting negatively, allow your adolescent to consider all options and keep the dialogue going. Help with the investigation of careers. Ultimately, respect that your adolescent has the final choice and show that you mean this. All careers should be a consideration, provided your adolescent doesn't say he wants to be something along the lines of a contract killer or a drug dealer. In this case you probably won't be responding, 'That's nice. Tell me all about it!'

'Okay. Whatever.'

Most parents lead very busy lives. However, there is surely nothing more important than your children. Always try to find the time to listen. If you are really too tired to talk something over, or to grapple with an important issue, it's better to be honest and to simply admit this to a young person. 'I've had a really rough day. Can we talk this over tomorrow when my brain is awake again? I'm too tired to make any sense right now.' Be honest with your adolescent. Most young people are fine with an answer like this. Also, if the topic raised by your adolescent is a really 'curly one', this tactic can buy you a little extra time to work out how you will respond. There are going to be times when you'll need this space to regroup your neurons to be alert enough to negotiate with a younger and more agile mind.

Make a definite time to get back to this discussion. If you don't do this, your adolescent may come to the conclusion that you just don't care. Find the time and place to show you do care.

'But you're doing so well at school. Why throw it all away? You can do better than that!'

This is almost guaranteed to make your adolescent defensive and angry. 'What would you know! You never listen to what I want anyway!' You could also be placing your child in a very unpleasant situation. Either he gives up something he really wants to do, or risks losing your approval. Most young people do actually care about what parents think and often desperately crave their approval. Listen in a nonjudgemental way.

'Great! Free haircuts!'

Lucky you! But now take time to talk things through.

summary

The tasks of adolescence

- To form a secure and positive identity
- To achieve independence from adult carers and parents
- To establish love objects outside the family
- To find a place in the world through career direction and economic independence

6

The ideal environment for raising an adolescent

Perhaps the biggest problem in adult/adolescent dynamics is that parents can attempt to impose the sort of control and authority exercised when children were pre-adolescents.

The key to establishing that *ideal environment* to nurture your adolescent is *connectedness*. This is a feeling of 'belonging', of feeling needed, of being an important and loved member of the family. It's the age-old notion of 'bonding'. A young person who has this feeling of connectedness, will usually have the strength and confidence necessary to face the changes and challenges of adolescence, and of life in general. Giving your adolescent this gift of connectedness is the best way you can protect them from the danger zones parents fear most.

> Kids need your presence much more than your presents.
>
> **Jesse Jackson**

A landmark study of 12 000 young people, conducted by the University of Minnesota in the United States, found that those with a strong emotional attachment to parents and/or teachers were less likely to take drugs, drink alcohol, have sex at an early age or engage in violence.

In an ideal environment, young people feel *safe, valued and listened to*. They are more likely to experience emotional wellbeing and to become resilient and happy adults.

It goes both ways

The one thing I decided when I had my children was that I would always be there for them. I'd be there when they came home from school. They're often angry or tired after school. I was a latchkey kid so no-one was home till late, and I just hated it. I don't necessarily have to say anything, but I'm there. Perhaps they're a little too dependent on me ... Chris tells me everything ... he's nearly eighteen. There have been times when I've spoken too quickly perhaps and then I've thought about it. Maybe I've said something inappropriate. I'll go back and apologise and explain why I said what I did. They know I'm human and that I make mistakes. It goes both ways.

Ingrid, mum of five boys

Help your adolescent to feel connected

- Establish good communication.
- Listen and be prepared to compromise.
- Accept that your opinion will not always coincide with that of your adolescent.
- Respect the opinions of your adolescent.
- Develop a good understanding of adolescence – be prepared!
- Have realistic expectations of your young person, especially regarding school results.
- Affirm your adolescent! Give praise when things go well, and find opportunities to praise.
- Feelings of security and 'belonging' are strengthened if someone is there when young people wake up, at meal times and when they go to bed.
- Make meal times an opportunity to be a family and to exchange thoughts and feelings. Adolescents feel that their lives are valued if they are encouraged to talk over what has happened during the day.

The Sunday roast

The main thing I like about my family is that we get together for dinner just about every evening. My sisters have moved out – they're older than me – but they come back for the family roast on Sundays. We talk about school and share ideas and I tell them about troubles like homework. They notice if something is going on. I had huge girlfriend troubles last year. They didn't ask me to talk about it but they asked, 'Is everything okay?'. It was good because I didn't feel I was on my own but they didn't break any privacy ... We'll watch the news together and opinions are always strongly expressed ... but not a lecture. Friends I know who don't get along with parents usually don't share meals.

 **Michael, 18**

Family is extremely important to adolescents. Young people who have a bond, a 'connection' with even one other member of the family, are much less likely to do anything to threaten that bond. Young people who feel loved are usually not so much at risk of depression or high risk taking. A connection with the family protects young people.

As long as you're happy

I think the biggest worry for teenagers these days is family. It overrides school, money, friends. If home was better for teenagers, lots wouldn't go out so often, they probably wouldn't get into trouble at school so often or do drugs. I don't know exactly what would make teens happy. Basically, I guess it would be a family that understands. What do we want? Support. A family that isn't hooked on reputation or looks and materialistic things. Parents who won't criticise you after the first sentence, the first word. Parents who don't assume, who don't jump the gun.

It's astonishing how many parents push their kids too much. Sometimes they push them to be what they themselves weren't. This makes the parents think that they are doing what's best for the kids when, in fact, they are making us unhappy and letting huge pools of anger build up inside. If some kids went up to their parents right now and said they wanted to become a plumber, the parents would have a heart attack. Teens would love it if parents said, 'We don't care what you want to do, as long as you're happy.' I've seen so many kids who are depressed because they can't live up to their parents' standards. Parents gotta be more understanding, more open to their kids' choices in life. And, no matter what, they should support whatever decision their kids make.

Teens should be treated as individuals. We hate being bossed around like slaves. There are so many parents who don't know their kids. They think *that they know them. If parents are not really listening then they don't know their teen as a person at all. That's why for some teens, friends are their family. They provide them with all that a family doesn't. Open arms and open ears. The best way to understand and support us is not to talk, but to listen. A teen who is uncomfortable at home will seldom be at home.*

Nam Hoang, 18

Home should be a place where the overriding message is that a young person is a valued family member. Take the time to tell your adolescents that you love them. Do not simply assume that they know this. Young people are constantly being bombarded with demands and expectations on all fronts. Home needs to be a place where the worries and stresses of fitting in and measuring up can be left at the front door. Home should also be the one place where a young person is sure that they will always be accepted, will always be listened to and where being loved is a certainty. This doesn't mean that home will always be a perfect, conflict-free zone. It should, however, be a place where a young person knows their voice counts.

School as a protective factor

Young people who see school as worthwhile are less likely to engage in hazardous, life-threatening behaviour. Try to ensure that, as far as possible, school is a pleasant experience for your adolescent. Some young people find a connection with school in areas other than academic. This could take the form of feeling valued as a team member in a particular sport or a member of any other school program. Support your adolescent in whatever activity they feel committed to. Adolescents need to hear the message that being involved and contributing is important, not necessarily winning or taking the lead role in the activity chosen. Young people with this security are less likely to become involved in high risk-taking behaviour. They are *protected* by the knowledge that they *belong* at their school.

A belief system or spirituality as a protective factor

Young people who have a belief system, who are spiritual, are also less likely to go off track. Research is showing that spiritual young people handle the stresses of life more successfully. Having a sense of connectedness to something that transcends the material protects young people because it can offer meaning when life is difficult, and comfort in the times when tragic events strike.

Parents don't have to rush out and join the family up to the nearest church. Simply having a belief system in things other than the material is beneficial. Young people should be encouraged to have a basic belief in life and its meaning and purpose. Parents are able to assist adolescents to believe in life by teaching them to first of all see meaning and value in their own lives. A large part of this involves ensuring that young people know they are precious members of their family. Parents can also lead by example in assisting their adolescents to appreciate life and to live life to the full. Young people who see their parents enjoying life and approaching life with optimism are more likely to have the same attitudes. Having a positive outlook provides a great sense of security for young people and helps to protect them during the difficult times.

Having a reason to live

In the United States recently, a young man was sentenced to life imprisonment. He told his psychologist he wanted to die. When asked why, he said, 'Because I will never be able to go to the mall again.' The thing that gave this young man's life meaning, was going to a shopping mall. Young people without purpose and meaning in life are more at risk because they tend to view themselves as existing purely in the material world. It is almost as though they have a hole in their soul that is easily filled by the dark side of youth culture.

> My experience is that these 'spiritual anorexics' don't naturally come to a sense of having limits on their behaviour. They have no place to stand emotionally when they are sad. It's about meaningless-ness versus meaningfulness. The message for parents is clear. Sacredness in a young person's life is a protective factor.
>
> **Michael**

Parents can also teach their children to be realistic and optimistic. Young people need to believe that while some things in life cannot be controlled, many are within their control. They need to hear that what is important is to reach out and give life a go. Parents who themselves respond positively to hardships and disappointments teach their children that what is important is to pick oneself up and to go on after a rough time. This valuable lesson provides young people with the security of knowing that they don't have to be *perfect*, only the best they can be.

Young people and spirituality

Spirituality is important to the health of young people. It assists them to find peace and fulfilment, and to establish their own life values and sense of meaning and purpose in life. It can take many forms such as participation in formal religious activities, a connection with nature experienced by a walk along the beach, or a time of reflection. But no matter how it is expressed, how can parents foster this sense of spirituality in their teenagers?

■ Engage in open conversation about the 'big' questions of life – belief in 'something' outside the material concerns of life. This may be a new and sometimes threatening experience for parents as we realise that we haven't got 'the answers' for these questions ourselves. Relax – you don't have to! Adolescents need to develop their own ways to deal with these issues. Leave the discussion open and encourage them to think for themselves. Encourage sharing of experiences that may be seen as spiritual, without ridicule or judgement.

- *Encourage ritual celebration of significant life events. Societies with a strong spiritual sense tend to be those where significant life events and rites of passage are celebrated with appropriate ritual – they are, in fact, recognised as sacred. This recognition can be extended to rites of passage such as reaching puberty, leaving school or leaving the parental home. Young people love ritual; even the simple act of lighting a candle to recall a significant person or event will usually meet with a positive response.*
- *Encourage engagement with nature. Many young people describe their spiritual experiences in terms of some sort of connection with the natural world. Encourage quiet times alone in the bush, times of silence and meditation.*
- *Encourage self-expression of spirituality through drawing, poems, dance. Encourage but don't force sharing of this.*
- *Finally, develop your own spirituality. If you are not on your own spiritual journey, you won't be much use to others on theirs. Nurture your own soul!*

Lynne Robertson, Chaplain

The big questions

There is a real yearning in young people to delve into issues like the meaning of life and death. Parents can play an integral part in supporting adolescents as they grapple with these questions by providing those experiences of the 'ritual celebration of significant life events'. Adolescents place an extremely high value on parental recognition. They love to have their families make special arrangements to celebrate a particular event or achievement in their lives. And they need to see that parents do recognise the milestones in their young lives and to actually hear the words, 'Good on you! We're proud of you!' These are the words and the memories that will sustain young people when the going gets tough. It's this level of parental acceptance and recognition that makes young people feel special and protects them from high risk taking.

A special person as a protective factor

Young people sometimes have a significant person with whom they have connected outside the family, and this also provides another important stabilising and protective factor for them. It is important for an adolescent to have someone to trust so that they do not feel alone and possibly overwhelmed by problems and changes.

Parents can help by encouraging their adolescent to become involved in activities or clubs to maximise their chances of meeting that someone with whom they will connect and feel able to turn to in tough times.

Parents can make sure that home is a good place to be, a place where young people know they will not be judged and evicted if they 'stuff up'. At the end of the day, the most significant people in the lives of most young people are their family members, in particular the parents. Feeling loved by the family is a huge protective factor for young people.

> You can't talk to your kids about sex and drugs if you can't talk to them about their music.
>
> **Greg Whelan**

What's that music?

" I walked into my son's bedroom when he was playing music that was quite tuneful and said, 'What's that music? It's really nice.' He replied, 'That, Dad, is Smashing Pumpkins.' Well, two weeks later it was my birthday. Guess what I got? And every time it came on the radio my son said, 'Dad, Dad, they are playing your song!', which was kind of nice. The cardinal rule of parenting is really to try to take an interest in what your children are interested in. Many, many young people respond really well to that. What I have learnt over time is that many parents have grown apart from their children. They don't know what they are interested in ... "

Michael

Protective factors for young people

- Connectedness to family – feeling safe, valued and listened to
- Stable family environment – real communication with parents
- Regular quality time with the family – meal times, family outings
- Positive experiences at school – not necessarily academic success but liking school
- Realistic parental expectations about academic performance
- Peer support – friendship groups
- Belonging to clubs or groups – sporting, musical, youth groups
- Having someone to talk to – a significant person
- Experiencing a sense of success in any area – academic, sport, a hobby, part-time job
- Positive outlook on life

Risk factors for young people

- Lack of connectedness to family
- Unstable family environment – family conflict or violence
- Parents rarely spending time with children – irregular meal times
- Lack of connectedness to school, negative experiences at school – academic issues, bullying
- Unrealistic parental expectations in regard to academic results
- Lack of peer group, friendship group
- Experiencing a significant loss or number of losses – a best friend, a family member, place in a sporting team
- Confusion over sexual identity
- Lack of any significant person to talk to, feeling isolated and alone

Respect

Sometimes the actions of parents are well intentioned but are, nonetheless, seen by adolescents as lacking respect. Adolescents are hypersensitive and they place a very high value on respect.

Family loyalty is important. Think carefully before revealing private details of an adolescent's life, even to a teacher or family friend. Avoid having such discussions in front of your child. No-one appreciates hearing their shortcomings detailed, especially in the presence of someone like a teacher. Young people want to be treated with respect and as young adults. The only way we can expect them to act in an adult manner is to approach them as young adults.

Parenting styles

Perhaps the biggest problem in adult/adolescent dynamics is that parents can attempt to impose the sort of control and authority exercised when children were pre-adolescents. If parents ask a nine-year-old to do something, usually the child will do it, often because the parent is physically bigger and smarter. Generally, parents can convince little children to do what they want. Adolescents are a million times more likely to question parental authority. They also have a burning desire for privacy of thought, action and deed. Parents, on the other hand, often want to know what their adolescent is doing every waking, breathing minute of the day. The way this conflict is handled is crucial. *Parenting style* is extremely important. Messages to our young people should be clear and not open to misinterpretation. Let's take a look at some parenting styles: what to adopt and what to avoid.

> Before I got married, I had six theories about bringing up children – now I have six children and no theories.
>
> **Earl of Rochester, 1647–1680**

The equality model

Some parents need to remember that *they* are the adults. Relating to your adolescents as friends and equals rather than as sons and daughters means you are not providing guidance. Young people are already preoccupied with challenges such as working out *who* they are and if they are *normal*, working at establishing friendships, deciding what's trendy, figuring out relationships and dealing with sexual attraction. In the midst of all of this confusion, parents need to provide stability.

Knowing that they have an adult there for support if the going gets rough provides security for adolescents. This does not mean that parents have to keep a distance between themselves and their children, and it doesn't mean parents have to be inflexible. It simply means that young people need to be aware that there will be occasions when the adult decision must be adhered to despite the fact that it differs from their own. This decision should be discussed with the young person and an opportunity given for the expression of differing opinions. If the process is seen as being fair, there is a greater chance that the final decision of the parent will be respected. It is important that young people don't see situations where opinions clash as being a contest about who will win this time. Parents need to explain the reasons for their decisions and show that they are decisions made out of a concern and love for the young person.

Avoid saying:

- 'You'll do it because I said so!'
- 'This is my house and what I say goes!'
- 'I don't have to explain anything to you!'
- 'Figure it out for yourself!'
- 'The answer is NO!'
- 'I have made my decision and that's that!'
- 'Get out of my sight! You heard what I said and the answer is still NO!'

Such statements will only cause further tension and animosity between parents and adolescents who, above all, want to be respected and listened to.

What you could say, after discussion and listening, and making your decision clear but, if possible, open to some compromise:

■ 'I understand that some of your friends go out to nightclubs but I really don't want you to go. I do trust you but I would worry myself sick in case anyone hurt you. I'm happy to drive you to parties and pick you up.'

■ 'You know that I don't want you to smoke because of the terrible effects on health. I really worry about you! I can't stop you from smoking but at least consider what I've said about the effects of smoking and please don't smoke in the house.'

■ 'We don't want you to leave school yet. We are worried that you'll regret this decision and you know how much we care about you. We want you to be happy. How about staying at school till the end of this year and then we'll have another talk about it all again.'

■ 'We do believe you when you say you won't try drugs again, but we have been worried sick about you! You are the most important person in our lives and we don't want anything to happen to you. We really want you to go along and talk to a counsellor. Please do this for us so that we won't worry so much and we know you are safe.'

Grabbing the reins

Fifteen-year-old son comes home and breathlessly announces that he has been invited to a party on Saturday night – not just any party, but the party of the year! It is, we are informed, the biggest, best and most important party of his life. Everybody will be there. Sadly for teenage son, there is a problem. The family has been invited elsewhere and the invitation has been accepted. The news is met with a stunned, almost disbelieving look followed by an outburst. 'You can't be serious! Are you mad? You just don't understand how important this party is! I have to go. I'll lose all my mates if I don't go. My life will be ruined!'

Normally this would be a fabulous time to negotiate a settlement with a win–win solution. In this instance, however, there is no room for negotiation. The invitation has been accepted. It's part of being a family. While this is a big deal for a young person, there will be other parties. This is one of the occasions when parents have to grab the reigns of parenting. Time to engage in some reality therapy. There is no evidence that missing this particular event will cause everyone to hate our son. If you stay calm, some of what you say will be heard, especially if you already have a reasonably trusting relationship with your child.

Michael

The head-in-the-sand model

Some parents bury their heads in the sand, preferring not to know what their adolescent is getting up to. Perhaps some react in this manner because the whole area of adolescents and adolescent behaviour is so frightening. Ignore it and it will all go away? Usually not. Ignore what is happening and you could be in for some real trouble! It's always better to be involved in the life of an adolescent and to be aware of what is happening in the life of that young person.

Patricia Hersch observes in her book on American teenagers that 'the fabric of growing up has been altered'. Hersch argues that today's adolescents have been left to their own devices by a preoccupied, self-involved, and 'hands-off' generation of parents. Adolescents have been forced to figure out their own system of ethics, morals and values, relying on each other for advice on such profound topics as abuse, dysfunctional parents, drugs and sex. Some adolescents are indeed 'a tribe apart', but not by choice.

It is essential that parents do not abandon adolescents at what can be one of the most confusing times of their lives. Parents need to be there for their adolescents. Career, finance and other issues are not as important as a young person's happiness. Problems and conflict between parents and adolescents should be faced and resolved, not ignored.

Avoid saying:

■ 'I sometimes think Andrew is on drugs but I might be wrong. I heard him telling Jason that marijuana is okay! God, what should I do? They might just be experimenting. Anyway, if I say something, I'll just make him explode again. Perhaps it will all sort out somehow if I give it time.'

■ 'I can't bear the fighting. It's better to say nothing. What's the point! Julie won't listen to me anyway.'

■ 'I wouldn't know what to say to Liz and Mike even if I had the time. I wouldn't know how to begin discussing things like sex and drugs. Besides, most kids sort all that stuff out for themselves anyway.'

It is very important to work at establishing good communication links with adolescents. Keep trying to talk because young people do want guidance. They may resist talking things over initially, and even appear not to listen, but if parents persist, their children will listen, eventually. It's better to bring things out in the open and risk a 'fight' than to ignore what is happening. All families fight at times. What is important is to minimise the number of fights and to maximise the listening to each other. If parents say nothing, they risk giving adolescents the message that they don't care. Sometimes things won't just sort themselves out unless parents take an active part. There is too much at stake – the wellbeing of a young person – to stand back and simply hope everything will come out okay.

What you could say, calmly, quietly, respectfully, but aloud:

■ 'I have noticed that lately you appear to be really tired all of the time. You're also losing a lot of weight. I'm really worried about you. Tell me, is there anything wrong?'

■ 'I overheard you saying to your brother Jason that marijuana is harmless. Can I ask you what you think about it?'

■ 'You know that if there is anything you want to talk about, I'm here for you. You've looked upset about something for a while. You seem really unhappy most of the time. Is everything okay?'

The kid glove model

Recent times have seen the creation of a culture of indulgence, where some parents seem hesitant to use moral language or set boundaries and limits for their adolescents. These parents appear to be completely and utterly bewildered by the challenge of parenting an adolescent and are frightened to make explicit their beliefs, values and expectations.

It is vital to enter into negotiations with adolescents around curfews, drinking, driving and other activities before they actually start going out. Once again, it is important to involve young people in these discussions about expectations and their rationale. This demonstrates not just that parents value their children's opinion, but also communicates that they care and increases the likelihood that the 'rule' will be adhered to. It's okay to tell your adolescent that you don't appreciate their behaviour as long as this is approached sensitively.

Setting boundaries won't necessarily mean that your adolescent will always adhere to them. However, the fact that you have laid down boundaries conveys to your adolescent that they are loved. This is a very valuable message for young people.

When those boundaries are not respected, it's important that young people learn to accept the consequences of their actions. This is teaching them about responsibility and also about picking oneself up after a 'fall' and getting on with life. If boundaries are discussed with young people and are considered fair, this is a valuable learning experience.

Spreading their wings

Being the parents of an emerging teenager presents challenges as she tries to spread her wings, to push the boundaries. We persevere, making decisions based on instinct and what we think is acceptable for her, regardless of what *'everyone else is doing'. While we are often seen as mean there have been times when we have sensed that she was grateful, almost relieved that we took a certain stand. We feel that if we give her too much freedom at thirteen, then the joy of turning fifteen or sixteen will diminish as she has 'been there, done that'.*

Anne Marie and Mike Minear

Avoid saying:

- 'I don't like you coming home at 4 a.m. and not telling me where you have been. I worry all night.'
- 'I'd really prefer that you don't swear all of the time.'
- 'Please tell me next time you aren't coming home for the night. I was going to call the police.'

It is important to set boundaries and to spell out consequences of not respecting these. Parents need to stand firm over the important issues. Young people need to learn to respect others and to understand the notion of compromise. It is important for parents to insist that young people do respect other members of the family. This does not weaken the important notion of unconditional love. Parents are not lessening their love when they have firm expectations. As long as young people are involved in discussions of these consequences, and they are seen as being fair, parents are doing young people a disservice by failing to remain faithful to them. Having firm and fair expectations can actually provide a sense of security for young people. The underlying message is that Mum and Dad do care!

What you could say, calmly but firmly:

- 'We really need to talk about last night. This is the first time you've come home at 4 a.m. without letting us know where you are. It has to be the last time, too. We care about you and all we ask is that you let us know what time you'll be home. We'd like you to call us if you are not going to be home by 1 a.m. We really want you to do this, otherwise we can't allow you to go out for at least a week so that you will remember next time. We think this is a fair request. What do you think about it?' This doesn't mean that you are backing down. It is just giving your adolescent the opportunity to make some comments, often along the lines of: 'My friends don't have to call ...' Your answer? 'We love you and care about you so we want to know where you are. End of story.'

- 'We have already talked about swearing. You know it upsets us to hear you talk like that. We care about you and respect your feelings. It goes both ways. Please don't talk like that again, otherwise, no going out for a week. Do you want to say anything?'

The Spanish Inquisition model

Parents adopting this model show little trust in their adolescents and demand to know everything. The effect of this strategy is to cause great resentment and to lead your adolescent to believe you don't trust them. Adolescents who feel they aren't trusted are usually very angry and are often reluctant to trust parents in return. While communication is fundamental to a good relationship with a young person, allowing your adolescent some privacy is essential. Rather than firing questions, a good approach is to allow time for a conversation to develop. Pick the right time to bring up a topic you are worried about, and, if the response from your adolescent is negative, choose your words carefully. Never demand that your adolescent talks something over and *never* intimate that you don't trust them. You can express your concern and then leave it at that. Perhaps a little space is needed before your adolescent is ready to talk.

Avoid saying:

- 'Where have you been? And don't you dare lie to me!'
- 'Don't you dare walk away! Get back here immediately! And don't answer me back in that tone of voice! Where have you been?'
- 'Who have you been talking to? What have you been doing? Look at the time! What have you been up to? Answer me!' (All in one breath)

Questions fired in negative tones usually only serve to anger and alienate adolescents. This is a very bad idea as it often angers a young person to the point where they will simply lash out at parents, and sometimes even deliberately engage in high risk-taking behaviour to prove they can't be pushed around. Despite the high level of frustration, it is better to say nothing until things have calmed down and the blood pressure is once again below danger level. A calm and positive approach is a much better way to go. Young people tend to 'switch off' when the volume of a parent's voice increases, and 'take off' when sarcasm enters the conversation.

What you could say, quietly and calmly:

- 'We haven't seen you much this weekend. What's been happening?'
- 'Please don't get upset. If you don't want to talk right now that's okay, but we just want you to know that we care about you and if you want to talk about what is upsetting you, you know that you can always talk to us.'
- 'Let's not talk right now because we're all upset and tired. How about we talk things over in the morning? Would you prefer that?' (No threat, no sarcasm)

The laissez-faire model

This approach, understandably, is very common in our busy world. Many parents fall into the trap of making spur-of-the-moment decisions. If parents are inconsistent in their expectations, adolescents are unsure about how to react and behave. The most dangerous result of such a model is that young people see inconsistency as being unjust. If young people lose respect and confidence in parents, this soon leads to situations where adolescents seem out of control. Parents need to clearly communicate expectations to adolescents and to engage in positive communication.

Avoid saying:

- Day 1. 'No! You are not allowed to go to that hotel under any circumstances!'
- Day 2. 'Are you telling me that you won't come to grandma's sixtieth birthday party if you can't go to the hotel? Look, just get out of my sight! Go if you're silly enough to get mixed up with those ratbags!'
- Day 3. 'You didn't tell us you would be getting home at 5 a.m! We just can't trust you to do anything right! You're grounded for a week!'
- Day 6. 'You want to go where? Look, I'm really busy tonight. I've got to finish this report … it was due yesterday … sure, sure … yes … have fun … ' (All said without looking up)

If parents are inconsistent, young people are more likely to spin out of control. They feel more secure if they know where they stand, and are familiar with the 'rules of the game'. They are also more likely to follow the rules if they are perceived as fair. An inconsistent approach from parents generally leads to a nightmare of a ride through the adolescence of their children. It sometimes takes a lot of patience to establish expectations, but this effort will usually be well rewarded. Teachers face this challenge with every new class. Young people like to test the waters and to see just how much they can get away with. Teachers learn that there is no quicker way to lose control of a class than to be inconsistent. The same applies at home. Young people soon work out what they can and can't get away with in handling their parents. Be fair and consistent.

What you could say:

- Day 1. 'We really can't let you go because there have been too many fights at that hotel. It's too dangerous and we don't want you to be hurt.'

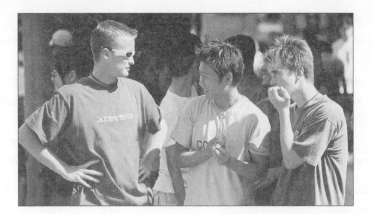

- Day 2. 'You're not going to your grandmother's party unless you can go to the hotel? She would be so hurt if you did that. This has nothing to do with your grandmother and you know how much you mean to her. We really can't change our minds over this one. How about you ask your friends to come over here? We don't mind if you go to a different venue, just not that one. Yes, you can go out to see a movie. Don't forget we agreed you will call us if you are going to be later than 1 a.m.'
- Day 3. 'We are really upset that you didn't come home until 5 a.m. You know that you agreed to call us if you're going to be later that 1 a.m. You also know that we have made it very clear that if you break this agreement, you won't be going out for a week. Please don't make us worry like that again. We thought something had happened to you.'
- Day 6. 'No, you can't go out. You know you can't go out again for at least a week. That was our agreement. Let's make this the last time we all have to go through this. Come on, cheer up. An agreement is an agreement. There aren't many days to go before the week is over.'

The perfect model?

There is no perfect strategy; it's often just about getting through each day as best as possible.

The major concern for parents should be to focus on preserving the relationship with their adolescents. Sometimes, this will mean trying a combination of strategies and despite all of the goodwill in the world, explosions will occur. At these times, it's all about hanging in there and riding out the storm. We all make mistakes. What is important is to keep talking to young people, keep telling them how precious they are and then be honest about having made hurtful comments or hasty decisions. It means going back to the drawing board and finding a workable solution for both parties. This can be an exhausting process, and parents need to be armed with lots of strategies and have someone to talk things through with.

Don't be afraid to set limits or boundaries. Most young people prefer to know where they stand as long as the boundaries don't arbitrarily change and they are seen as being fair. Before you make a huge statement, think carefully about how this will go down with your adolescent. Will it simply alienate your child more? Is there any other approach you could take? Would it be better to wait until the air clears and then try to talk things through?

A dad's thoughts

We have five boys aged from five to sixteen. You sense if your kids are happy or not. Right now we sense that we have to keep an eye on Michael, for example. There are times when one of the boys needs us more than the others and then we find the extra time for them. Helen has always been at home – always there when they come home from school, as they go through the multiple bowls of cereal and toast. That's when you learn what's going on.

If there are conflicts, we try to be diplomatic. If the kids fight, our policy is, 'You just don't touch. No hitting.' We speak privately to the kids and they each understand what they can and can't do. When circumstances require it we speak to all of the boys together. We tell them that their behaviour is not acceptable and that if they have frustrations, they must come to see either Mum or me. They know that punishments will follow if they don't listen. This will be something like cleaning the kitchen. Now, cleaning up after a roast dinner for seven people is not a flash job!

We try to have dinner together as a family, and it's a family tradition that each person mentions three things that happened over the day. Our fifteen-year-old, Matthew, particularly enjoys this. It's his moment. He's in the limelight. Recently he had to choose subjects at school and talking at dinner means that it becomes a family matter. It's not easy but we try to find time for the kids. We have four basketball games every Saturday and Matt has footy on Sunday. We see each of the games and, if they clash, Helen and I go our separate ways – as long as one of us is there for each game!

We're upfront about drugs and things like sexual activity. Helen has been instrumental in making sure the family watches television programs on these topics. At the dinner table we also have discussions from time to time. The kids tend to push the boundaries from our point of view. And then, well we have to rethink our 'policy' from time to time. We're starting to get used to this idea. We question things and sometimes we need to change. We have to try and respect the boys. It's brought us some serious discussion, but persistence has paid off. We're a close family.

Mark Bourke, father of five boys

A recipe for parents of adolescents ...

Take a big helping of communication (above all, listening), mix gently with sensitive negotiation, frequent demonstrations of interest in your adolescent's interests and, then the final ingredient, lots of love!

The cook needs to be patient, however, as the mixing requires time (sometimes quite a few years) and the ability to forgive, laugh and trust. The laughter part is an essential ingredient and may sometimes require 'time out' for the cook to recharge the funny batteries! But the end product of all of this effort will be absolutely delightful! Not even Michelangelo could create something as incredible as a new young adult!

It's hard not to overreact. We all lose it at times. It's a good idea to approach an adolescent a while after there has been some huge scene and say something along the lines of being sorry for blowing up. You will often be in a position of advantage because your adolescent will be caught unawares, probably expecting a scud missile not a peaceful approach. Take the opportunity to explain why you were so upset or angry (avoiding any hint of anger, sarcasm or blame) and to try talking things through.

This does not mean you have to back down or give in. There may be room for compromise. There may not be. What's important is to tell young people why you feel the way you do and ask them how they feel. One of the responses most hated by young people is, 'Because I say so!' If you believe what you said previously can't be altered, calmly explain why. However, if after consideration you believe you did go a little overboard with whatever your expectations were, you won't be losing face if you modify these expectations. Your child will probably respect you for being honest and fair rather than being too stubborn to change anything you initially stated. You aren't giving in. You are being fair and rational. You are communicating in the best possible way, with all cards on the table, with real honesty.

Avoid saying:

- Anything you don't mean, or anything hurtful, threatening or sarcastic.
- What you could say: 'I'm sorry I said what I did. You know I love you. I was just angry and I'm sorry.' (A great approach)
- 'We want the best for you. You are a terrific person. We love you … ' (Be positive)

After giving everyone a chance to say how they feel, it's great for parents to allow a young person to move on in a positive way:

- 'How about we forget what's happened and make a new start!'
- 'Pizza, anyone?' (Food is always a good way to round off a 'deep and meaningful' or a clash of opinions.)

Survival tips for parents

Just as adolescents need someone to off-load problems on, the tougher the going gets, the more important it is for parents to also have a significant person to confide in. Handling everything alone is stressful and exhausting, and makes it more difficult to keep things in perspective. If this person also has adolescents, comparing 'the latest' can not only be reassuring, but, more often than not, result in both parties having a much-needed laugh. Parents need time out occasionally. This may only be a few hours, but everyone needs time to relax and to recharge the batteries.

If things degenerate to the point where the situation seems hopeless, the time has come to talk to a professional. No situation is ever hopeless. A counsellor may also suggest that some form of counselling would be helpful for the adolescent too. It's not a good idea to battle on alone.

Spending time together

My family gets along well because we have a strong family bond. Mum and me, we argue, but we end up laughing. I've just turned eighteen and I'm the youngest. I have three brothers and the eldest is twenty-six. We still have some little fights about clubbing. My mum and dad are worried there might be fights and people doing drugs. But I can do more stuff like going clubbing because I am the youngest. They've given up! They've got over the stress. Every week the whole family goes out once to dinner and we talk and laugh a lot. I reckon there is a shield between you and your family if you don't spent time together.

 **Michael, 18**

One day at a time

Recently a friend of mine, Karen, told me about a frustrating experience with her sixteen-year-old daughter, Tania. Karen heard the doorbell ring and went to the door. She found her daughter's friend waiting while Tania grabbed her bag, so Karen chatted with the friend until Tania arrived.

'So, you're off to see a movie? That's nice. What are you going to see?'

Suddenly Tania arrived and silenced her mother with a chilling look, and a clear signal to 'butt out'. Much later that night, Tania arrived home banging and slamming things around, giving a very obvious signal that she was furious with her mother. Finally, her mother asked what was wrong. 'Do you know what really pisses me off? Why do you have to be so nosey? You're always checking up on me!' Karen assured her daughter that she was simply making polite conversation with her friend to make her feel welcome. Tania stormed off. Next time, I'll just stay in the laundry, Karen thought.

We talked about how touchy adolescents can be, and how precious privacy is to them. But, what's the solution? Karen feels unwanted. Tania has the perception that her mother doesn't trust her. We decided it would be a good idea for Karen to approach her daughter quietly when it had all cooled off. She would reiterate, in a nonconfrontational tone, that she was genuinely just making conversation with the friend. It wasn't a 'find out what's going on' interrogation. Karen already knew they were going to a movie. I convinced Karen to simply act normally the next time a friend of her daughter arrived, and to continue whatever she was doing. There was no need to bolt for the laundry. Adolescents are naturally hyper-sensitive and defensive about their actions. Perhaps her daughter had simply had a bad day. Of course she didn't want her mother to disappear from her life. There would probably be lots of other occasions where she would welcome her mother's help, picking her up or allowing friends to stay over. There would be many opportunities for Karen to show that she did welcome her daughter's friends in the house and that she wasn't simply doing some detective work on the side.

Erin

Parents need to talk things through calmly with adolescents and not to overreact or panic when there is a conflict or misunderstanding. Disappearing will only allow the distance between parents and their children to grow. During late adolescence, young people change almost daily. One day they want parents around; the next, they appear to resent their every word, however innocent. What needs to remain constant in the midst of all of this is that adolescents feel parents will move on after a conflict, that each new day can be a new start, that the love of the parents remains unchanged.

CRUNCH TIME

Setting boundaries!

On which of the following issues is it most important to stand your ground?

- Tidy room
- Loud music
- Curfews
- Homework

Tidy room

This does seem to worry many parents. But, if you think about it, does it really matter as long as the door is kept shut and you don't think strange animals or insects have moved in? There are bound to be more serious issues to focus on. Save your energy for the big battles!

Loud music

While this can be annoying, it's probably not the most serious worry on this list. It is important, however, to discuss something like this with your adolescent and to calmly present your thoughts. There should at least be a compromise made. Adolescents do need to be guided to learn consideration for others in the house. Negotiate! Compromise! Get them earphones! But don't give in!

Curfews

This is a serious issue because most parents spend too many sleepless nights waiting for their adolescents to return to the nest. When a 'return home time' has been agreed upon, adolescents should stick to this and should be aware of the consequences of not doing so. There is a greater chance of success with this if your adolescent has been involved in the negotiation of the set time. Consider being open to discussing exceptions to this such as end-of-year school parties. Young people need to be given the opportunity to learn and demonstrate responsibility and consideration for others. Make your rationale for the curfew time clear. You worry about your adolescent and care about their safety.

Homework

While this is an important issue, it's probably not going to give you the headaches missed curfews will. Talk over homework problems with your adolescent and see if you can help out with the work itself and also in establishing good homework routines. Homework first, television later? Homework first, phone and email friends later? Talk these issues over with your adolescent and demonstrate your interest.

summary

The ideal environment for raising adolescents

- Connectedness through feeling needed and a feeling of belonging
- Feeling safe, valued and listened to both at home and at school
- Being prepared to compromise
- Having realistic academic expectations
- Fostering optimism and spirituality

CHAPTER 7

Communication with adolescents

It's hard to really communicate with someone you don't know well. How well do you know your adolescent?

Young people need to feel that they are trusted. Many, given the chance, will live up to our expectations. And it's great for parents to be able to talk openly and honestly about when they were young and how they felt. This also shows a high level of trust. Young people who can communicate with their parents are much happier and more secure. Honest communication is a high priority for young people.

> The rules for parents are but three ... love, limit, and let them be.
>
> **Elaine M. Ward**

Hear your kids

A problem for kids is that, for many adults, kids don't have voices and aren't very mature. Lots of adults don't believe children. They'd rather just listen to the adults' side of the story. When a teacher or adult asks you to explain to them your side of the story, you know there's no point and you can talk about mermaids for all they care because they don't listen to you anyway.

My parents would have to be the worst case of having deafness towards their kids, especially me. My parents don't believe anything I say. They really don't understand me nor where I'm coming from. When I get in trouble at school, and the vice-principal tells them something totally whack, my parents believe him over me, despite cross-examining me for about two hours. My parents simply don't believe me, nor in me. I've given up. Every day I try to please them and to make them happy, but I always stuff up. I try to get good grades at school and do, but when the slightest problem occurs, they hold it against me until the next problem arises. I really don't care any more. I just can't wait till I'm like nineteen or something, so I can do whatever I want. I give my parents the utmost respect. I do everything they say and I do everything for them. When I see other kids mistreating their parents, I tell them off. I'm here because of my parents and for them, but they don't understand that. I've given up.

 Robbie, 17

Tell them they are forgiven

"
Robbie was fifteen when he was asked to leave his high school, several months after he wrote this journal entry. He is now seventeen and talks about his current life situation.

Erin: How are things with your parents now?

Robbie: The same. I got suspended from school two years before I wrote that journal entry. Dad lost it! After that, they always referred back to it. They see me as this little boy who goes off the rails. A nutter.

Erin: Did you try to do anything to change things?

Robbie: Plenty of things. I got a part-time job. I wanted to be independent. I've stayed with the job for two years. I once came home with a really good exam mark. They didn't say anything. The past has to come up all the time. 'You've hurt us so much ... ', they say to me all the time. I just sit there and wait for the lecture to be over. Once we were in a restaurant when they started on all of that. I put my head down on the table. They say I've hurt them. They don't have the thought that I could be worrying. I was hurt too.

Erin: So you don't feel that you are trusted yet?

Robbie: No way! I come home and I can tell they've been going through my things. I got so angry that I went through their room. Bad mistake. I found a letter my mother had written to her sister but hadn't posted yet. She said that I was the biggest disappointment in their lives ... Sometimes I even have the dinner cooked when they come home from work but they don't say anything. I'm going to leave home as soon as I can.

Erin

When adolescents make mistakes

- Forgive and move on.
- Don't dredge up the past.
- Notice the little things and give praise where praise is due.
- Respect the privacy of young people.
- Listen.

Let them taste life

My parents are really liberal and they have always trusted me. Where things between us have been a bit uncomfortable, they've always made the effort to open up the dialogue. I think that's important, even if it's a bit scary sometimes. A lot of parents go into denial. I think that burying the head in the sand is a bad approach. Deep down they know what's going on but they don't want to admit it. Sometimes I've asked to do things that now, looking back, were ridiculous. When I was about fifteen, I wanted to go to a nightclub! My parents said something like, 'We don't think it's a good idea, but if you really want to go … '. Did I go? Yeah! It was awful! Dreadful!

My parents have also been honest about their past. Dad told us he used to sneak out at night to play in a band. A lot of parents don't tell their children about the stuff-ups, the stupid things they did. My parents have often joked about their experiences, and that makes it a lot easier to relate to them …

Natasha Stojanovich, 20

The need to trust

If parents show children that they are trusted from an early age, most do measure up to these expectations. It's a wonderful experience to see the proud expression on the face of a young person who has just been entrusted with carrying out an important task. Teachers see this all the time. The eager hands shoot up. The faces are beaming out the message, 'Choose me! Choose me, please!' And how much more precious is the trust of a parent than that of even the most respected teacher. It's disappointing to see adults expecting the worst from young people. It must be very frustrating, even infuriating for young people in this situation. Some simply give up and live down to the expectations of the adults around them. We would all find it hard to always be presumed guilty.

Of course young people are going to disappoint at some time, just as parents will invariably disappoint their teenagers at some point, too. We all like a second chance. Extending the same to your adolescent may just pay off in ways you never imagined. Being able to say, 'Let's forget what's happened; we all make mistakes,' allows the relationship with your teenager to continue as it was, or sometimes to become even closer because your teenager will appreciate you showing that you can move beyond what has happened. Young people often say that once they make a mistake, Mum and Dad never let them forget it: 'What's the point trying to do the right thing if your past mistakes are continually thrown in your face?' or 'What's the point trying if you are never given the opportunity to prove you can be trusted again?'. Ensure that you are always open with your adolescent and prepared to forgive mistakes and to move on. Good parenting is focused on the present. Don't be the world's worst archaeologist. Adolescents hate it when parents dig up the past.

> The art of dealing with children might be defined as knowing what not to say.
>
> **A. S. Neill**

> The face of a child can say it all, especially the mouth part of the face.
>
> **Jack Handy**

Rules for dealing with conflict

- Pick the right moment – cool heads are best.
- Be conscious of your tone of voice, facial expression, demeanour and body language.
- Don't overreact or underreact (Good luck!).
- Don't accuse, insult or talk down – attack the problem.
- Focus on the present – not the past.
- State your feelings (no whining, and skip the martyr routine).
- Listen attentively and get the facts.
- Acknowledge your adolescent's feelings, experience and point of view.
- Don't try to control or win – give and take and negotiate.
- Arrive at a solution.
- Rest up for the next encounter.

Establishing and improving communication with your adolescent

- *Pave the way for a more pleasant time during the adolescent years by establishing communication with your children from an early age.* (The day they are born is a good starting point!) You're going to strike trouble if you are just starting to communicate with your children when they hit adolescence. You are now competing with raging hormones and more interesting friends. Good luck! You're now dealing with an unknown quantity who doesn't understand what is going on, who you are … and you want to 'chat'?
- *The good news is that it's never too late.* After all, you do pay for the food and we know that adolescents are really hungry almost all of the time! It's not a good idea to mention this, though; adolescents generally don't respond well to blackmail or sarcasm. Just keep plenty of food in the house and be patient. Resist the temptation to yell back and eventually some of what you say will get through.

■ *Choosing a good time and a good place are important for getting the communication ball rolling.* If, for example, your adolescent loves tennis or there is an event you could imagine sharing with them, organise a day out and see if you can strike up a conversation. It will eventually happen even if it takes a few attempts. Give it time. It's probably not a good idea to suddenly organise an activity you can share with your 'scary' adolescent, and in the middle of the finals of the tennis, lean across and ask a 'heavy' question. 'So, what do you think about sex?' The people sitting around you may or may

TANDBERG

not be amused by your shocked or annoyed adolescent's reaction. Build up to the more serious issues and questions.

- *Keeping calm when conflicts arise is important for maintaining communication with young people.* Not reacting to angry outbursts from an adolescent is extremely difficult to do. It might help to keep in mind that the outburst might be caused by hormones temporarily in possession of the mind of your young person. Also, young people give out very mixed messages. On the one hand they tell parents that they need and expect help in providing them with food and a nurturing environment, and on the other hand they say, 'Look, I can run my own life! Butt out! Get out of my face!' Keep in mind that these displays of 'I'm in control!' often camouflage intense feelings of insecurity and confusion.

Disarmed

According to our thirteen-year-old son, the middle-aged teaching couple who are his parents are 'decibel-hypersensitive' and just plain boring. This young chap comes from a very sophisticated generation. On one memorable occasion, when I had mustered a tirade to hurl on this fragile little person, he asked with an unnerving philosophical calm, 'Dad, do you love me?' Bewildered, I dismantled my armoury of verbal abuse (at least I don't nag) to answer in the affirmative. 'Of course I love you.' 'Then why would you want to hurt a person you love?' The moment was defused and I bowed to his superior intelligence.

Andrew, father of two teenagers

- *Finding time to apologise and rebuild bridges is essential.* If you are drawn into an angry exchange of words – and it happens at some point, even to the most patient of parents – and you 'lose it', get 'it' back! 'Losing it' should be avoided if possible, because feelings are hurt or sometimes adolescents actually enjoy the show! They've won! Picture siblings saying to each other, 'Watch this!' and then pressing all of Mum's buttons at once! Mum explodes, doing a commendable imitation of Mount Vesuvius, and little has been gained.

- *Sometimes, it's better to walk away.* If you've searched the deepest recesses of your mind and no positive words and responses can be found, walk away. Don't attempt to talk when your blood pressure is going through the roof. You're likely to later on regret what you say. It's okay to go into your bedroom and to scream quietly into the pillow. Time out!

- *Don't leave issues unresolved.* After you have cooled down – and, hopefully, so too has your beloved adolescent – come back and try to talk things through. Don't leave things up in a very unpleasant air. When you do talk, your tone of voice, facial expression, demeanour and body language are all important. About 70 percent of what you communicate to adolescents has nothing to do with what comes out of your mouth but a lot to do with your overall approach. Approach as if you were about to dismantle a bomb or a landmine. Watch where you place your feet!

- *It's a good idea not to talk too much.* Sometimes it's better to say nothing. Adolescents complain frequently about being nagged or lectured. So, resist the temptation to yell and avoid the evangelical preaching approach. Don't whine, and forget the martyr routine. Adolescents have heard it all before! *An effective tactic is to speak only two sentences at a time.* And try not to raise your voice. The average adolescent has an attention span of about 13.6 seconds when it comes to listening to parents.

- *Get the facts.* Adolescents frequently complain about parents not listening. Listening attentively is a very powerful strategy for maintaining communication.

- *It is okay to 'lose' a few arguments with adolescents.* Remember, it's not about winning. It's okay to concede the minor issues, but remain firm on the big ones. Acknowledge your adolescent's feelings, experience and point of view though.

- *Use humour.* It's a fabulous tool! Remember, *the parent who laughs, lasts!* Keep humour upbeat, never sarcastic.

- *Never accuse, insult or talk down to a young person.* The moment parents use sarcasm or put-downs, defensiveness is triggered in adolescents and productive communication is over. One of the nastiest habits a parent can have is to resort to character assassination. The message parents need to give is *'I love you, but I can't stand your behaviour.'* Communication and connectedness go out the window if personal attacks are used.

■ *Only argue over things that matter.* Let some things go by. Don't comment on everything. Adolescents hate this. Save your energy for the big stuff! This means that when you do argue over the important issues, they are more likely to take notice. Despite this, many parents say that it's the small things that drive them crazy. If you want something to change, discuss *why* you want this, and the consequences of this *not* being followed. Some things simply aren't open to discussion because they adversely affect other members of the family – usually the parents – and consequences simply need to be clearly spelt out and followed through.

Behaviour modification

We had lots of clothes being left around our home and I called a family meeting. Our children sat there muttering, 'God, Dad's doing his psychology thing again.' I said, 'This is very simple guys. Your mother and I are not your slaves and we are not going to pick up after you. From now on, any clothes left around in public areas will be put in this cardboard box and it will be locked in the garage for one week. That's it. Got it?' Of course we had hysteria and some people had to go to school without their uniform and got detentions. You have to stick to what you say. In three weeks' time though the public areas were pristine. Simple! Basic behaviour modification. Anyone can do it.

Michael

■ *Avoid confrontations or ultimatums.* The moment you issue a young person with ultimatums one of two things will happen. They will take you up on it and then you've really got trouble, or you have to back down and you lose credibility. Don't paint yourself into a corner. There are more effective techniques you can use. Don't ever forget you are the adult and can develop a whole range of strategies.

■ *Regularly give positive feedback.* One of the most important things in the world is that young people receive some form of praise. The latest research suggests that the average adolescent receives one positive message for every five negative messages from parents. In schools, it's one positive for every ten negative messages. It's great if you can catch your adolescent doing something you can praise. Never miss an opportunity. There will, eventually, be something.

It's the thought that counts

A few months ago I was heading off on one of those really early morning starts. I crept out of the house at 5 a.m. and noticed that my son had remembered to put the garbage out. Asking the cab driver to wait, I tiptoed back into the house, grabbed one of those little yellow 'post it notes' and put a message on my son's door: 'Christopher, thank you so much for putting the garbage out. Wrong night, but nice try.'

Michael

- *Don't remind adolescents of their past mistakes.* Allow them to move on. Dragging up the past only causes resentment and anger and absolutely strangles communication. Focus on the positives.

Choose words carefully

We have three daughters. They gave us a hard time, especially the eldest. She started early wanting to do this and wanting to do that. It was hard. We were under a lot of stress. There was always fighting. Then one day we found the eldest in her room smoking. We didn't allow smoking. We said something like, 'Look, you either abide by the rules in this house or make other arrangements.' And she did! It broke my husband's heart. We never thought our kids would leave home. I still can't go down into her room. We really didn't think she would leave. We didn't mean for her to leave. I think there was also a lot of peer pressure for her to leave. For several years she moved from house to house living with different friends.

Before she left, I know I'd fly off in a temper, but she used to drive me to boiling point. My husband was very ill at the time – we nearly lost him. I used to fly off. The eldest would start going on about things and we were too tired to discuss things then. We did the best we could; we didn't know what else to do. We gave them love. They didn't come with a book of instructions. We did our best. Anyway, now, five years later, our daughter who left has moved into a place just around the corner – walking distance! I babysit her dog!

Sophie, mum of three

At times, all parents say things they don't mean. And, despite all of the love in the world, things don't always go the way parents want. When life is busy and there are additional stresses like illness in the family, it's essential that parents take time out to rest up and get things in perspective. Raising an adolescent requires endless energy. When mistakes are made like saying things not really meant, parents need to sort out the misunderstanding with their adolescents. The most important message of all is that the young person is loved and valued by the family. As long as this message is understood, while it may take time to heal wounds, that bond between parents and children remains.

Good communication

- Avoid sarcasm.
- Remain calm.
- If angry, walk away, choose a better time.
- Listen, then talk.
- Never accuse.
- Focus on the present.
- Only worry about the serious issues.
- Be prepared to 'lose' some arguments.
- Avoid ultimatums.

It's hard to really communicate with someone you don't know well. How well do you know your adolescent and contemporary youth culture?

- Do you know the names of your adolescent's best friends? Have you met them?
- If your adolescent stormed out one day after an argument, where do you think they would go? Do you know where your adolescent's best friends live? Which one would you eventually call if they were missing? Do you have the number?
- Is your adolescent happy at school? Why/why not?
- Do you know the subjects your adolescent is studying and the names of their teachers? Have you met them? Which ones do they like or hate? Why?
- Do you know the types of books, movies and sporting identities your adolescent likes?
- What is your adolescent's favourite sporting team? Favourite type of music? Musical group? Television program?
- Do you know if there are any particular topics, issues or hobbies that interest your adolescent?
- If your adolescent plays sport, do you know which position they play on the team? When was the last time you went along to watch them play?

- If your adolescent has a part-time job, have you met the employer?
- If your adolescent hasn't got a part-time job, would they like to find one? Could you help out with suggestions or with preparing a résumé?

If you don't know the answers to these questions, make time to find out. Taking an interest shows you care.

Emergency strategies

If the situation between you and your adolescent is so volatile that the family dog actually prefers to sleep in the garage, consider some of these suggestions:

Make a peace offering

You don't have to take out a loan. In fact, don't go overboard. It is, after all, the thought that counts. So, this could be as simple as a box of your adolescent's favourite chocolates. Leave it in their room and you might consider attaching (no, not a device that explodes upon opening!) a carefully thought-out note or letter. Perhaps all you need to write is something along the lines of, 'I do love you. How about we go out for a pizza? Let's talk things over when we feel better, and less hungry! How about it? Or I could order in a pizza if you have a lot of study tonight. What would you prefer? I'm sorry I shouted.' Who could resist a note like that attached to a little peace offering – plus the offer of food? Worth a try.

> After a good dinner one can forgive anybody, even one's own relations.
>
> **Oscar Wilde**

Find a go-between

Try talking to someone your adolescent seems to listen to. This can be tricky because you don't want this to backfire and seem as though you are going behind your adolescent's back. Make sure you can trust this person to be very diplomatic. The intention is to strengthen the relationship you have with your adolescent, not to further damage it. If your adolescent is involved in a particular activity such as sport, music or a youth group, there is often a significant person, an older person your adolescent respects, involved in these activities who would be a good person to speak to.

It is a good idea to know which adults your adolescent obviously admires. Often adolescents will talk a lot about these significant people, and parents need to listen to these important conversations. These are often the people who have the wisdom and experience necessary to sit down and chat with your adolescent about life in general. A sensitive person is often able to somehow introduce the topic of family issues without even alerting a young person to the fact that this has been initiated by the parent. If you choose the right person, this can be a very successful way for your adolescent to see things through the eyes of a 'neutral' person.

Call a family meeting

It's important to choose a time when fireworks are not exploding. Rather than bringing up any negative examples or focusing on any particular issue, make the message very positive. You are concerned about the tension in the house and want this to change. You care about every member of the family and want to see everyone happy. Ask for suggestions. It's a good idea to state that all suggestions must be positive. You may be surprised at what you will hear. Listen carefully. Every member of the family should be able to present their feelings regardless of their age. Sometimes even very young children have interesting and helpful thoughts about difficult situations in the family.

Allowing each person to speak validates the worth of each family member and teaches adolescents the importance of respecting different views. What is important is to make each person feel valued but at the same time responsible for the harmony in the family. Adolescents often respond well when they appreciate the rationale behind family decisions. This is often far more effective than parents imposing decisions on young people. If it seems impossible to reach a compromise to which all children will agree, however, they need to realise that this is when the parents' decision must be respected.

Seek advice

Sometimes it may be necessary to seek another opinion. A professional counsellor can help to put things into perspective. While friends can offer invaluable advice, if you believe that there may be something seriously wrong with your adolescent, it is important to obtain advice from experts in the area of adolescent health and wellbeing.

Listen

My parents are very strict. They won't let me go out clubbing and they won't even listen to my side. I wish they'd at least listen.

Sue, 17

Talk

Parents can't impose their views on you ... I find if we disagree on anything, they say their bit then I say my bit. Then we discuss it ...

Tim, 17

The young are always ready to give to those who are older than themselves the full benefit of their inexperience.

Oscar Wilde

TANDBERG

How to increase conflict

- 'Get this room cleaned up right now! You act like you were born in a pigsty!'
- 'You call this a report? A baboon could do better! You'll never amount to anything!'
- 'I can't believe you could be so stupid! At your age I was out working and bringing up two kids.'
- 'Why aren't you like your sister/brother? I'm not wasting any more time on you.'
- 'After everything we have done for you! I'll never trust you again!'
- 'You've never appreciated what we've given you. You're more trouble than you're worth.'
- 'Don't lie to me! I know you're on drugs! You've always been a disappointment!'
- 'It's cost us a fortune educating you and this is how you repay us!'
- 'How could you do this to us? You're a disgrace to this family! Get out of my sight!'
- 'You've been trouble since the day you were born! I suppose you're happy now.'
- 'You enjoy hurting your mother/father/us, don't you!'
- 'I knew this would happen! Are you crazy or something? Grow up!'

All guaranteed to produce anger, humiliation, frustration, rebellion and even despair in your adolescent!

How to defuse conflict

- 'We're all getting upset. Let's leave it and talk later.'
- 'Let me see if I've understood. You feel … '
- 'Don't forget, I'm on your side!'
- 'Let's finish the argument now, but I want you to have the last word.'
- 'I'm really sorry I shouted at you. How about we try to sort this out without hurting each other's feelings?'
- 'I don't know what to say. What would you like me to do?'

- 'I know you're upset. Don't worry, we'll sort this out.'
- 'Let's forget what's happened. We all stuff up sometimes. The important thing is that we're both sorry about what has happened/what we've said.'
- 'Let's not fight any more. I don't like seeing you so unhappy. Let's see if we can find a solution that we're both okay with.'

All worth a try. But if none of these work, you should seek professional advice.

Let go of the trivial

> In arguments with young people, the trivial has to go. There is always a parent who says, 'Oh look excuse me, I know you were talking about those really serious things like suicide, eating disorders and depression, but can you tell me how I can get my daughter to keep her room tidy?' My answer? 'It's very simple. Does her room have a door?' 'Yes.' 'Use it.' 'Oh, are you suggesting I just shut the door?' 'Yep.' 'But it smells!' 'That, Madam, is why the good Lord gave us air freshener. Seriously, unless the Health Department comes and puts a yellow ribbon around the place and declares it a toxic waste dump, don't worry about it. She has to live in it, not you, and it is just not worth it. Do you really want to spend every waking moment of your day worrying about whether she lives in a tip or not? It's a totally different matter for general parts of the house, public spaces ... but, as far as the bedroom goes, shut the door!'
>
> **Michael**

Adolescent espionage

> Discovering what's going on in a young person's head is far more important than what's growing under the bed. Recently, one of my students began to behave in an aggressive and disruptive manner. His work took a nosedive and he was in trouble with almost every teacher. Taking him aside after class, it didn't take long to

work out what was causing all of this. He didn't hate school, he hated the entire world, and especially his parents.

Paul told me that his parents didn't trust him. They were convinced he was involved with drugs although he assured them he wasn't. After becoming suspicious that his room was being searched, he elaborately arranged certain objects in drawers and could immediately see what had been touched. He had the 'evidence' and was furious. His privacy had been invaded. To make matters worse, Paul's parents then denied searching his room. All positive communication with them had been destroyed and he was in the process of planning a suitable revenge. Underneath the anger, I could see a great deal of hurt.

An adolescent's room is their castle, and privacy is extremely precious to them. They resent parents barging into their rooms unannounced. Although they often won't show it, young people desperately need the trust of their parents. Searching through your adolescent's room is not a wise approach if you hope to maintain their trust and respect. I tried to convince Paul that his parents were acting like this because they cared about him and probably even regretted searching through his things. He needed to hear this from them, too.

Erin

Conflict!

What is the best response if your adolescent swears at you?

- ☐ Swear back. Show who's boss
- ☐ Say you won't accept this language and ground them for at least a month
- ☐ Explain why you don't want this language and discuss consequences if it happens again
- ☐ Threaten to wash their mouth out with soap if it happens again

Swear back. Show who's boss

Tempting, but not a good way to go. It's a good idea to lead by example, so don't swear back. Anyway, do you really think you could keep this up for eleven, twelve, fourteen years? Adolescence officially kicks off with the beginning of puberty and can last until your adolescent turns 21, 22, 25! You'll have a much nicer life if you can manage to communicate calmly with your adolescent and diffuse anger. Find a good time to discuss your feelings about being verbally abused and outline what is and isn't acceptable. Set clear expectations and clear consequences for breaking these. Ask for your adolescent's views, too. By listening to their feelings, you might even find out why they are so angry.

Say you won't accept this language and ground them for at least a month

As a parent you are definitely justified in not accepting this behaviour. However, it's a good idea to give a warning first. Try to involve your adolescent in the discussion and avoid using a 'You'll stop it or else' tone. Adolescents don't respond well to threats. A calm discussion and clearly set out expectations usually have a greater chance of succeeding. You might also like to think about the punishment fitting the crime. One month's grounding may be too harsh for swearing when you consider the whole host of other more serious mischiefs a teenager can get up to. You may not want to get into a situation where your adolescent is grounded for the rest of their life.

Explain why you don't want this language and discuss consequences if it happens again

Yes! Calm approach. Clear and fair expectations. No sarcasm.

Threaten to wash their mouth out with soap if it happens again

While this might be possible when your adolescent is ten or eleven, this will be a little more difficult when they are older, and taller, and bigger! It's much better to establish open and positive discussions when children and adolescents are younger and to establish workable boundaries or 'rules'. You set the expectations and conditions. One warning? Three strikes and you're out? As long as your adolescent clearly understands where they stand, you are safeguarding yourself from being labelled unfair.

summary

Communication with adolescents

Good communication is based on:
- Trust between parent and child
- Openness and honesty
- Being able to forgive and move on
- Respecting privacy
- Avoiding sarcasm and put-downs
- A sense of humour and willingness to praise
- Letting go of the trivial

8

Relationships, sex and questioning sexuality

It's important for parents to initiate a discussion of the whole area of relationships with their adolescent rather than simply forbidding them to have sex.

Many parents find the whole area of adolescent relationships and sex very worrying. They are often embarrassed and unsure about what to do and say. Some say little, hoping that these areas will be taken care of in health education classes at school.

> You can tell a child is growing up when he stops asking where he came from and starts refusing to tell where he is going.
>
> **Unknown**

And, while it is generally true that most young people do receive some formal education about relationships and sex, parents do need to be involved, too. The good old 'birds and bees' talk is still necessary, but at a much more sophisticated level than ever before.

Starting early

Today's adolescents generally reach puberty earlier than previous generations, and this 'maturity' is usually accompanied by an eagerness to taste life. This eagerness also extends to wanting to develop relationships and sometimes to experiment with sex. Many adolescents do not practise safe sex. Research also shows that more adolescents today are having sex than young people their age did in the past, and the average age of first intercourse is lowering.

Young people are naturally curious and most are far more aware sexually than young people even five to ten years ago. They watch movies and television. They surf the Net and they read magazines. All of these can contain sexually explicit material. If parents watched some of the programs popular with adolescents, they might be in for a shock or two. Popular programs show adolescents in 'serious' relationships, tossing up whom to go out with in one episode, and whether or not to have sex in the next. It's very romanticised and dressed up to give the message: 'This is what you should be doing. All people your age are! If you haven't, what's wrong with you?'. In addition to this pressure to have a relationship, young people are tending to question their sexuality at an increasingly early age.

Failing to measure up to peer expectations to find a partner can result in a young person being labelled a 'loser', or other hurtful terms. This can be a very stressful time for adolescents, a time when understanding and sensitivity from parents can help enormously. In the midst of all of this pressure to establish a relationship and to 'go all the way', the more knowledge adolescents have, the more they are effectively equipped with reliable and safe options.

Parents need to come to terms with the fact that their adolescents may experiment with sex. Discussing relationships and sex with your adolescent does not mean that you are approving of or consenting to them having sex. Initiating a discussion, however, does demonstrate that you are concerned about your adolescent's welfare. While parents cannot effectively forbid their adolescents from experimenting with sex, talking about the issues is important. You are demonstrating that your adolescent is a valued member of the family and that you care about them. This is a positive message, so long as it is part of a two-way discussion and not a 'Don't do this and don't do that' speech. Show that you are interested in your adolescent's world and listen to their views.

There is evidence to suggest that the **more** parents discuss relationships and sex with their adolescents, the **less likely** adolescents are to go out and have sex. Interesting! Is it because adolescents are completely 'freaked out' over the fact that a parent would bring up what is often a taboo subject, or is it that they are simply being guided to think things through more rationally and begin to consider all the possible implications of a sexual relationship? Either way, it is a good idea to bring up these important issues with adolescents.

Approaching the issues of sex and sexuality

There is no one perfect approach to suit each adolescent. Because of the early maturing factor, perhaps a discussion could be initiated early on, even before the onset of puberty. Parents can generally judge when their young person begins the growth spurt and will also notice the mood changes that usually appear around early adolescence. If possible, it's a good idea not to make too big a deal of this talk. Lessen the embarrassment for all concerned as much as possible. One possible start is to say you are aware that most schools talk about relationships and sex and that you are interested in what has been said at school. In most schools these topics are covered in health education, science or personal development. Many young people may prefer to pretend that nothing has been said or try to brush aside the whole thing: 'I know all of that stuff, Mum and Dad.' Try to keep the discussion rolling by asking a question something along the lines of: 'What was said at school about relationships? Sex? What do you think about it all?' Lead into the most important message: 'We care about you and need to know that you are safe. We know that there is often a lot of pressure to get a boyfriend or girlfriend and we want you to know that you should try not to let anyone put you under unfair pressure. Take your time. You know that you can always talk to us.' Try to ascertain if your adolescent is well informed, and therefore less likely to be placed in unsafe situations.

Talk things over

It's important for parents to initiate a discussion of the whole area of relationships with their adolescent rather than simply forbidding them to have sex. This is a positive approach and should take place at a carefully chosen time. This conversation could be particularly successful if it arose when the issue of relationships was featured in a program popular with young people. By openly acknowledging that there is a lot of pressure on young people to have a sexual relationship, parents are displaying their understanding and support. A discussion like this will only be productive if parents are willing to be completely honest. Young people are very intuitive and can detect when parents are being evasive with their answers or are unwilling to respond to questions. Parents should be prepared to answer questions and not simply ask questions. What is the best response when your adolescent asks you what age you were when you first had sex? The only good answer is an honest answer. Honesty in a situation like this is displaying a high level of trust in your adolescent. It shows a great deal of respect for a young person who is approaching adulthood and is dealing with adult issues.

Sleeping over

The issue of boyfriends and girlfriends sleeping over also needs to be addressed in an open and calm manner. Parents who avoid these discussions often place themselves in a very difficult situation. Bursting into the room of a young person will almost always cause a very angry response. First of all this is a denial of their privacy and can place everyone in a very embarrassing situation. The relationship between parents and their adolescent will most certainly be damaged and it is difficult to heal the hurt this action will cause. By bringing up this issue at a time when everyone is calm, parents have the opportunity to explain their feelings and thoughts rationally. This is a time when opinions may differ and parents should acknowledge this without judging their adolescent. If parents clearly make their feelings understood in a positive and nonjudgemental way, most young people will respect this. They desperately want their parents to acknowledge that they are growing up and also want to feel that they are listened to and respected. The best way parents can do this is to talk things through openly and to avoid an eruption of emotions.

Treat relationships seriously

Take the relationships of your adolescent seriously. For generations there have been jokes about 'puppy love' and 'teenage crushes'. Relationships are usually enormously important to adolescents, and negative comments or teasing from families can cause real distress.

It's likely that your adolescent will, at some time, be very upset by a broken relationship or an attraction that is not reciprocated. This is when parents need to offer sensitive support. Flippant comments will only further hurt and alienate your adolescent, and failing to take a broken relationship seriously only invalidates their feelings. It's not a good idea to say: 'You'll get over it! There are plenty of fish in the sea!'. For your adolescent, this can be a devastating experience. Your sensitivity is essential. We all remember that first love or crush.

Important messages to give young people

- Relationships should not be forced, unpleasant experiences. Young people need to hear what good relationships involve: mutual respect, honesty and trust. They also need to be reassured that it's okay to say 'No' to sex. It's okay to take time. Many are under the misconception that everyone their age has had sex. They need to hear that this is incorrect and that they should not be put under pressure by others who often simply boast about their so-called exploits.
- Young people need to be alerted to avoiding unsafe situations. Are they aware of how dangerous it is to hitch-hike? Do they know the safe alcohol limit? Are they aware of the dangers of unsafe sex? These types of situations should be discussed openly with parents without implying any lack of trust in the young person. Alerting them to potential danger shows that you care about them.
- Parents need to communicate that they would never reject their adolescent if they were gay. Adolescents need to know they can always rely on the unconditional love and acceptance of their family.

Worst case scenarios

For some parents, discovering that their adolescent is having sex or has contracted a sexually transmitted disease are shocking revelations. The news that a daughter is pregnant or that a son has just fathered a child at the age of fourteen is also very unwelcome. These are the times, however, when parental acceptance and support are most needed. Adolescents don't need to hear that they have been 'stupid'. They need to hear that their parents will help them and that they won't be rejected or continually reminded of this 'mistake' for the rest of their lives. When such serious issues arise, parents may also need independent support from friends or professionals to deal with the sadness, anger and shock that they may be feeling. Parents need to be strong to be able to support their adolescents through such difficult times.

Unwise reactions

- To hit the roof
- To blame your adolescent for being so stupid
- To disown your adolescent … to throw them out of the house
- To walk away in disgust
- To threaten

Wise reactions

- Remain as calm as possible.
- Don't blame or use accusations.
- Help your adolescent to assess all options.
- Consider independent and professional counselling for your adolescent and offer to accompany them.
- Offer support and understanding.
- Ensure that your adolescent understands they are not alone and will never be abandoned by you. You will work through this together.

What's going on in my adolescent's head?

It's normal and very common for adolescents to go through a period during which they question their sexuality. It's not uncommon for adolescents to have a same-sex experience during this time. This could be a simple kiss, or the relationship may progress further. A same-sex experience does not necessarily mean that a young person will eventually identify as being gay. Many adolescents go through a period of uncertainty during which they experiment.

For many young people, this can be a traumatic and guilt-ridden time because of the social stigma attached to homosexuality. Many have nightmares and believe that if they rush out and find a partner of the opposite sex, their feelings of being attracted to the same sex will all go away. Many engage in lots of heterosexual sex just to prove to themselves that they are 'normal'. Remember that wanting to be normal is one of the greatest concerns for adolescents.

Young people who are aware that homosexuality is considered a capital crime in the eyes of their parents are at risk of depression, high risk-taking behaviour, self harm and even suicide. Keeping in mind that it is common for young people to at some stage question their sexuality, and perhaps as high as one in ten will ultimately identify as being gay, it is important that parents have some knowledge of this issue. How parents react can literally be a life-saver for some young people.

TANDBERG

Young gay people

At a time when needing to belong and to be normal become enormously important, many young gay people:

- Experience intense loneliness, have no genuine sense of connection with anyone. They believe that no-one really knows how they feel and are afraid of possible rejection from friends and family
- Face homophobic comments and harassment on a daily basis in schools
- Often can't find other young gay people for support. It's difficult when many are also hiding behind a veneer of heterosexuality. This increases loneliness
- Fear being thrown out of home if they tell their family they are gay
- Have access to few positive gay role models and find forming a positive self-esteem difficult
- Feel so depressed and guilty that a high percentage engage in risk-taking behaviour – drugs, alcohol, sex – anything to forget for a while or to feel less afraid
- Find it difficult to concentrate in school or to sleep so results often take a dive
- Are high achievers who bury themselves in study to avoid facing the fact that they are gay
- Are afraid of 'discovery' so avoid talking to their parents
- Don't have access to much positive information about being gay and are very frightened
- Become socially withdrawn and avoid close contact of any kind
- Hide themselves among lots of 'friends' yet feel completely alone
- Believe that suicide is the only solution to a problem that seems overwhelmingly hopeless. Research suggests that as high as 25 to 40 percent of young lesbians and gays have attempted suicide, and that 65 to 85 percent feel suicidal

No more secrets

Midway through high school is often a stressful time for students. So my wife and I were not overly surprised that our youngest son was not his normal, cheerful self. A disinterest in school and the quiet, somewhat withdrawn change to his personality might also, we thought, be partially due to the comment he had made that he didn't seem to have too many friends at school that year. This did surprise us a bit as he was normally very sociable and confident with lots of friends.

One evening, during dinner, he made a quiet comment that there was something he wanted to tell us. As parents, we have always believed it is of the greatest importance that all channels of communication are kept as open as possible. When we asked what was on our son's mind, he suddenly left the dining table and ran to his room. We followed. What we found was unexpected and disturbing. Our son was in a darkened room, curled up in a fetal position, sobbing deeply. For a while he just couldn't, or wouldn't speak. We thought, Has something happened, or has someone done something to our son? After shaking his head to these questions, my wife asked quietly, 'Does it have something to do with your sexuality?' This brought an affirmative nod but continued sobbing and no words spoken by him for quite a few minutes. During this time both my wife and I lay on the bed next to him hugging him and softly telling him over and over that we were thankful he had told us, that we still loved him and that we would always be there to support him.

After what seemed a very long time, his sobbing died away and he began speaking, still in a fetal position. He said that for some time friends had urged him to 'come out' to us, but they told him to be prepared with contingency plans to stay somewhere else that night if he had to leave home. We realised that the crying and fear were probably due to uncertainty about our reaction. Now that he knew he still had a home and a family who loved him, he was able to tell us that he had been confused by his feelings about his sexuality for several years and had wished along the way that he could just feel 'normal'. We then understood why the year had been so difficult for him. We felt closer to our son than perhaps ever before. It is so important to talk with our children, not to be judgemental of them and to reassure them that we will always love and support them.

As parents of a gay son, we felt a great sadness to realise that our son had had to carry, even for a short time, the emotional uncertainty about whether or not he would be pushed away from his family for something over which he had no control. We are so pleased that he was able to come out at a young age and not carry the burden of living a secret year after year. One of the best things that we did soon after this day was to follow up on the information our son had given us and to attend several meetings of P-FLAG (Parents and Friends of Lesbians and Gays). We then supported our son in his decision to move to a new school as he told us he had felt some harassment at his current school.

It has been over two years now since our son came out to us. He has just graduated from his new school and actually enjoyed his final years. Our understanding and support have allowed him to accept himself. Like any other teenager, he's had highs and lows, but basically he's a relaxed and happy kid again.

 Adrian

What parents should know about adolescents questioning sexuality

- It's normal. A same-sex experience does not mean that your adolescent is necessarily gay. Let your adolescent know that you are not homophobic. There are opportunities to respond positively if gay characters appear on television, or the topic somehow comes up. Let your adolescent know that your love is not conditional upon them being heterosexual.

- Adolescents soon realise if their parents have a problem with this issue. Parents who do find this a difficult area to understand need to do a lot of reading and thinking. A negative attitude can devastate a young person. Young gay people comprise as much as 30 percent of completed youth suicides and are overrepresented in statistics for depression, self-harm, substance abuse and homelessness.

- If you think that your son or daughter may be attracted to someone of the same sex, don't panic! This may simply be an adolescent crush. Young people need the space and freedom to work it all out without the worry that you will disown them and kick them out. And, given the space, they will sort it out.

- If an attraction proves not to be a one-off crush then remember that your adolescent should be happy and be able to live life to the fullest. For a young person, nothing is more important than being accepted by the family. The realisation that the feelings of being attracted to someone of the same sex are not going away can be the most traumatic factor in an adolescent's life. It is important that you are there for your adolescent when they need you.

- There are many negative stereotypes about being gay. Parents need access to the facts in order to be able to support their adolescent if they are confused about sexuality. A person is either born gay or not. Being gay is not a choice. Many gay people talk about feeling 'different' from a very early age – some even during primary school.

If you think your adolescent is gay

▨ Relax and get some reliable information and support.

▨ Find a subtle way to bring up the topic and see how your adolescent reacts. If they appear to be homophobic, this is not an indication of whether they are gay or not. Adolescents often hide their feelings until they feel safe enough to 'come out'. Show that you would never reject your adolescent. You may be throwing a lifeline to your child.

▨ Don't ask outright unless you really feel the timing seems right, and you are prepared for any answer. It's a very difficult question for a young person to answer honestly unless they trust you. Letting your adolescent know you are okay about the issue is a great start.

▨ You are not alone. There are many information and support groups for parents of gay people. Organisations such as P-FLAG (Parents and Friends of Lesbians and Gays) have regular meetings where parents and friends of gay people can meet to offer each other mutual support. P-FLAG also organises social events so that gay adolescents are able to meet same-age peers to decrease feelings of isolation and to increase self-esteem.

▨ Remember, your adolescent deserves the chance to live an honest and happy life. Sexuality is just one part of a person. Your adolescent is still the same person regardless of sexuality.

TANDBERG

CRUNCH TIME

The sex thing

What is the best response if you believe your adolescent might be feeling pressured to have sex?

- ☐ 'Look, I'll be honest. It's not as good as it's cracked up to be!'
- ☐ 'Are you crazy? Wake up! You're not old enough to think about anything like that!'
- ☐ 'I guess you talk about this sex stuff at school. Want to order in a pizza tonight?'
- ☐ 'Don't let people push you around. You don't have to do anything you don't want to do.'

'Look, I'll be honest. It's not as good as it's cracked up to be!'

This isn't a helpful response. Peer pressure for young people to become sexually active can be heavy. This is the important issue to focus on. Discussing ways to deal with pressure would be helpful. Encourage your adolescent to find like-minded friends and reassure them that lots of young people who do boast about their sexual exploits are, in fact, not sexually active. While you can't control what is said outside the home, you can offer your understanding and support at home. Sometimes this is all that is needed to make a huge difference to the life of a young person.

'Are you crazy? Wake up! You're not old enough to think about anything like that!'

Avoid sarcasm at all times because it can damage the relationship with your adolescent. The whole area of sex is discussed frequently by adolescents and even by younger children. They are thinking about it. They live in a world where sexual images are all around them, even in television ads for ice-cream! It's great if you can discuss this whole subject and make sure your adolescent isn't worried or upset about it.

'I guess you talk about this sex stuff at school. Want to order in a pizza tonight?'

Nice side step, but this isn't going to help your adolescent with what can be an extremely worrying issue. These days, it usually isn't necessary to go into the mechanics of what goes where. Most young people receive sex education at school, which is a relief to some parents. What your adolescent may want to hear, however, is reassurance that they aren't 'weird' if they haven't become sexually active.

'Don't let people push you around. You don't have to do anything you don't want to do.'

Yes! It's important to first acknowledge that peer pressure is real and not an easy thing to deal with. Adolescents need to hear that they have the right to make their own decisions. They need to hear that they don't have to become sexually active until they feel ready and that they don't need to prove anything to their peers, boyfriend or girlfriend. Parents can help greatly by conveying to their adolescents that boyfriends and girlfriends who put that kind of pressure on them when they aren't ready don't have their best interests at heart. Be supportive.

summary

Relationships, sex and questioning sexuality

- Adolescents today reach puberty earlier than previous generations
- Start discussions early and listen to your adolescent's views
- Be aware of any school sex education programs
- Treat adolescent relationships seriously
- Communicate your acceptance of homosexuality
- Consider professional counselling if necessary

CHAPTER 9

In case of emergency

Don't blame yourself for everything. Don't blame your adolescent entirely, either. For every problem, there are many possible solutions.

No matter how carefully you parent, you will be extremely fortunate if, at some time, you won't feel as if you have been swallowed up in a big black hole. This is the time to pick up the pieces, to act in a positive and constructive manner, and to

> Accidents will occur in the best-regulated families.
>
> **Charles Dickens,** *David Copperfield*, **1850**

take time out. Time to distance yourself, to relax and then be able to return and confront problems in a calmer and more positive manner. Don't blame yourself for everything. Don't blame your adolescent entirely, either. For every problem, there are many possible solutions.

Let's look at some of the biggest parental nightmares and identify some ways to avoid these, and also helpful strategies and ways to react if the situation arises in your family.

The areas of great concern are:

- Adolescent depression
- Youth suicide
- Eating disorders
- Drugs

Depression in young people

The good mental health of adolescents is extremely important, and parents need to understand the difference between feeling sad and being depressed. We all have good and bad days when we experience the ups and downs of life, the joys, disappointments, failures and successes. Some young people and parents describe themselves as being depressed when they are simply having a 'down day'. What they really mean is that they are feeling disappointed, upset or sad. Feeling sad or unhappy may be an appropriate response to a situation. These feelings should only last a very short time – usually hours or days – and will not interfere with day-to-day activities in a major way.

Depression, however, is a diagnosable and treatable illness. Depressed adolescents need professional help. They will show some recognisable physical, mental and emotional symptoms and parents need to be alert in order to recognise them. They also need to be aware of the seriousness of a young person becoming depressed and be prepared to respond appropriately.

- Depression brings intense distress, which does interfere with an adolescent's ability to cope with the ordinary demands of living. Everything begins to suffer: self-esteem, health, school, homework, recreation and relationships.
- Symptoms of depression don't last only for a short time but generally for a prolonged period of at least two weeks. This is always the minimum period to warrant the diagnosis of depression, which must always be made by a professional.
- Adolescents suffering from depression are very difficult to be around because they are either really withdrawn or very irritable and annoying.
- Parents need to be alert and notice any persistent signs of change. For example, has a once-outgoing young person become significantly withdrawn and antisocial?

- If parents suspect an adolescent is depressed, they need to do more than tell them to 'cheer up' or 'snap out of it'. If parents don't seek immediate help, the adolescent's life could quite possibly fall apart.
- Depression is the most frequently reported mental illness, with rates having risen sharply in the past ten years.
- As much as 18 percent of children and adolescents have been found to have mental problems.
- Many adolescents suffering from depression are not treated because their symptoms are mistakenly assumed to be normal 'adolescent stuff'. Parents can't afford to turn a blind eye to the possibility that their adolescents may be depressed.
- Young people who have depressive illness are three times more likely to use alcohol regularly and to binge drink. They are also three times more likely to smoke marijuana on a weekly basis and three times more likely to engage in unsafe sexual practices.
- A young person with depressive illness has negative views of themself, their environment, family, school and, of course, the future.
- Between 60 and 90 percent of young people who attempt to take their own lives have a history of depressive illness.

Signs of depression in adolescents

These are some questions parents can ask themselves in order to work out if a young person may be depressed. They are all possible signs of depression.

Is your adolescent:

- More tearful than in the past or complaining of feeling blue or empty inside?
- No longer enjoying the things that used to give them pleasure?
- Spending more time alone, away from former friends?
- Gaining or losing weight?
- Looking more worn out and tired than in the past?

- Suddenly failing subjects or skipping classes and no longer a good student?
- Moping around and no longer their normal self?
- Suddenly and inappropriately irritable, anxious, violent or destructive?
- Inclined to describe their life as hopeless when something goes wrong? Red alert!
- Sometimes talking about death or suicide? Red alert!
- Self-harming? Red alert!

If your adolescent is continually 'down' and has five or more of these symptoms for at least two weeks, they may have a major depressive illness. This is depression, which requires professional help immediately. Organise to have your adolescent assessed.

Most schools either have psychologists, counsellors or staff who have special training in working with young people. In most communities there is also access to mental health services. Contact professionals and services that specialise in working with adolescents. These are the experts who can ensure that a young person receives appropriate counselling or treatment if necessary.

Many adults misdiagnose adolescent depression as simply being 'adolescent moodiness'. Depression is not a normal part of growing up, nor is it a character flaw or a sign of weakness. Depression can be successfully treated and an adolescent can recover fully.

Young people and suicide

Most of the studies in this area have looked at whether media stories on individual suicides increase suicide in the general population. While still controversial, there is good research suggesting that media reports of individual suicides, celebrity suicides, television dramas and even documentaries on suicide are all associated with elevated rates of suicide. There are, in addition, claims that exposure of young people to large volumes of information on suicide, stories, games and discussion groups on the Internet may encourage suicidal behaviour. The evidence for this is summarised in a report commissioned by the Mental Health Branch of the Commonwealth Department of Health and Aged Care, Australia, released late in 2000.

This report states: 'publicity about suicide may have unanticipated effects among vulnerable individuals who may model their behaviours upon the accounts of suicide presented by the print media and television'. The report goes on to say that media hype about suicide may increase its occurrence by 'normalising' the notion of suicide in a population, so that taboos that have previously surrounded suicide may be lessened and suicide may be more widely perceived as a common and acceptable option for people under stress.

Parents can help to protect their adolescents from thoughts of suicide by talking about how much they care for their children. If young people feel valued and loved, they are much less likely to want to end their lives.

Signs of suicidal tendencies

- Similar to the signs for depression, with the added factor that many young people who may be suicidal often give away possessions, draw pictures or write about death and dying.
- Parents need to be particularly vigilant if a young person is self-harming, talks about being useless or a burden to others, or talks about wishing to be dead. Parents must pick up on these signals and sit down and talk things over with their adolescent. Professional help is also highly advisable.
- There is clear evidence that many young people who take their lives have left many clues. They have actually mentioned to one or more people that they would be 'better off dead' or that everyone else would be better off. Comments like this should never be ignored. A young person who makes such comments needs to know that they are precious to the family; a lot of reassuring talk needs to follow.

■ Parents need to be alert if a young person who has been 'down' for a long time suddenly, and without any apparent reason, seems very happy or carefree. Unfortunately, this sudden happiness is sometimes the result of a young person feeling relieved because they have made the decision to take their life. Parents must immediately talk to the young person and seek professional counselling if they believe the young person is suicidal.

The facts about youth suicide

■ Youth suicide is often attributed to depression, sexual abuse, drug abuse, family break-ups or confusion over same-sex attraction. While any one of these factors can be enough to lead a young person to take their life, some young people are struggling with more than one of these.

■ Sometimes it is not one serious factor or event that leads a young person to want to end their life. A series of small, but disappointing events, can build up a picture in a young person's mind that the future is hopeless. Parents should know this and communicate their love and concern to their adolescent if they are going through a 'down' period where a lot of things seem to have gone wrong. It's very important to talk things through with a young person, and not just hope that things will all sort themselves out.

■ Some young people are very good at hiding their depression, so parents need to be observant.

■ Research now suggests that one in seven children can experience depression before the age of fourteen years and that many young people go undiagnosed and untreated, with devastating consequences for the individual, their family and the community.

■ In young people, death by suicide has tripled since the 1960s. Significant rises in suicide rates among young people, especially young men, is a growing international trend.

■ It has been estimated that for every completed male suicide, there are between 30 and 50 suicide attempts.

■ For every completed female suicide, there are between 150 and 300 attempts.

■ Deaths by suicide are more common among males; however, self-inflicted injuries have risen more significantly among young women aged 15 to 29 years.

■ For every completed suicide, there are at least 100 young people who attempt to take their own lives but do not succeed. This is a terrifying thought.

■ A better approach than talking about suicide is to focus on increasing protective factors for young people. Above all, connectedness to family is a protection for young people.

What parents can do

Effective suicide prevention strategies include increasing the social and emotional competencies of young people such as problem solving, decision making, anger management, conflict resolution and assertive communication. Parents have the ability to assist their adolescents to develop these characteristics and skills by:

■ Showing them trust and involving them in decision-making

■ Relating to them in a calm and rational way and teaching anger management by example

■ Establishing good communication and working through problems with them

■ Allowing and encouraging them to express opinions and to listen to alternatives before making decisions

■ Ensuring they feel valued, loved and listened to

■ Ensuring they are aware that nothing can alter parental love and acceptance

■ Looking for opportunities to teach young people how to deal with disappointments or 'failure'

■ Giving the message that we all go through negative experiences and what is important is to focus on the positives

Never leave loose ends

Sister: Are you sure you don't want your DVD collection anymore?

Kaz: Yeah, take it. Take those too if you want (pointing to a pile of clothes).

Sister: Gee, thanks. (Picks up gifts, comes out of the room and runs into mother)

Mother: What are you doing with Kaz's new clothes? She hasn't even worn them.

Sister: She gave them to me! The DVDs too.

Mother: (Enters Kaz's room) Kaz, what's going on? Are you all right? You don't seem yourself lately.

Kaz: I'm fine, Mum. I'm just tired. I don't want to go to school tomorrow. Maybe you guys would all be better off without me.

Mother: Don't be silly. Have a sleep and you'll feel better in the morning. (Leaves the room without addressing the issue)

Always make every attempt to encourage your adolescent to open up and talk about how they are feeling. By giving away valued possessions, Kaz is making a cry for help. Never walk away without saying that you are worried and emphasising how important your adolescent is to you.

Scott comes home looking sulky. He walks into the living room where his parents are watching television.

Mother: What's wrong, Scott?

Scott: Nothing. I'm going to bed.

Mother: But you haven't eaten anything. It's not even seven o'clock.

Father: Leave him alone. He'll grow out of it. This moody stuff, it's just a phase.

Mother: But he's acting kind of strange lately. Losing his job and then his girlfriend must be upsetting for him.

Father: Just leave it. It's only a part-time job and he should be studying more anyway. He'll have to get used to things not going his way, won't he. It's just part of growing up.

Scott has recently faced two very disappointing events and his parents may be unaware of other worrying issues he is facing. Events that, for adults, may not seem overly serious, can be earth-shattering for an adolescent. Having lost a job and his girlfriend, Scott needs to feel that he is not alone. This is precisely the time when he most needs time and reassurance from his parents.

With young people committing suicide each week, and countless others engaging in acts of deliberate self-harm, we must all play a part in preventing this silent epidemic. Youth suicide is best understood as a behavioural outcome, the end point of a 'journey' that may begin in many different places. Several risk factors increase the likelihood that a young person will end their life; however, the problem is that these contributing factors carry unequal weight. No one single factor has ever been demonstrated to be responsible for the suicide of any one young person.

The good news is that parents, schools and the community can play a major role in preventing mental health problems by helping to target one of the major risk factors in youth suicide: depression.

Schools can play a significant role in preventing depression in young people by introducing depression awareness programs where students are taught that depression is not a normal part of growing up, nor is it a character flaw or a sign of weakness. By teaching young people that depression is a group of symptoms with observable mental and physical signs different from just feeling sad or blue, the chances of early detection and intervention is significantly increased. Schools also need to reward young people for social involvement, to promote connectedness to school, and to teach skills such as conflict resolution, anger management, problem solving and assertive communication. Students need to be taught to name and to recognise thoughts and feelings in a nonjudgemental atmosphere.

Ultimately, however, the greatest responsibility for the wellbeing of young people lies with parents. Adequately informed and equipped to recognise changes in a young person's behaviour, parents can play a substantive role in youth suicide prevention. Changes in behaviour and signs of distress must be taken seriously. Early identification of possible depression is important. Parents must listen and, if necessary, encourage the young person to see a health professional. While the demands of the modern working world can be incredibly draining, nothing is more important than the mental health of our young people. Parents can make the difference.

Young people and eating disorders

Eating disorders are psychological illnesses that can potentially have very serious physical and social consequences.

The most common eating disorders are anorexia nervosa and bulimia nervosa. They can be treated, and early identification is important to minimise damage and increase the likelihood of recovery. Parents can play a key role in working to prevent an adolescent from developing a serious eating disorder. Noticing early signs and acting immediately can prevent 'bad habits' and negative thought processes from developing into potentially life-threatening illnesses.

What is anorexia nervosa?

Anorexia nervosa is basically self-imposed starvation. The person affected often has problems with body image. Despite being a healthy weight or even being very thin or emaciated, sufferers see themselves as being fat. A person with anorexia often restricts food intake to the very minimum while inducing vomiting, taking laxatives and diuretics and engaging in strenuous exercise. This cocktail of body abuse results in severe damage to a person's health.

What is bulimia nervosa?

Bulimia nervosa sufferers also have a great desire to lose weight and an equally great fear of putting on more weight. They tend to have periodic compulsions to eat large quantities of food and then to induce vomiting at the end of each eating binge. They find themselves caught up in a dangerous and vicious

cycle of dieting and binge eating, which leads to feelings of anger, guilt and failure, followed by purging and feelings of self-disgust, guilt and depression.

What causes young people to develop eating disorders?

There are many possible causes and no single cause. Some risk factors, however, appear to make some people more likely to develop an eating disorder. These are some of the signs to look out for and some suggestions about how to handle what can be a frightening situation.

Dissatisfaction with body image

This is a huge issue for many adolescents. Many are unhappy with their appearance, and a diet can develop into an obsession to lose more and more weight and then become an eating disorder. Unfortunately, this problem is becoming more common in children even before they reach the adolescent years. Children as young as seven have been found to have high levels of body dissatisfaction. In one study, 20 percent of very young girls and 18 percent of very young boys tried to lose weight at some time. Four percent were actively engaged in extreme weight control.

What parents can do

Parents need to be aware of this frightening trend for children and adolescents to obsess about weight. If young people often make comments about their weight, the weight of friends or people presented in media images, try to pick up on this and talk things over. Knowing the facts about the health dangers of extreme diets is important. Ask a young person how they feel about the whole issue. Parents can also lead by example and focus attention on healthy eating and keeping fit rather than starving to achieve a certain weight. Discussing healthy recipes and healthy activities is a positive start. The whole family can become involved in planning meals or (miracles do happen) perhaps even cooking these culinary delights. Suggesting that sport and other activities rather than diets are a good way to keep fit will hopefully not only keep young people fit physically, but may also have other benefits such as providing opportunities to make friends or for the family to spend time together.

Media images

These constantly reinforce the belief for many young people that thin is in. Models, actors and television personalities admired by young people are often so thin they are becoming increasingly difficult to see unless the viewer has 20/20 vision or strong prescription glasses. Young people are constantly confronted by articles about weight loss and how to achieve the 'perfect' body. It is not surprising that many adolescents are becoming casualties of a media assault that focuses too much attention on the body beautiful and sells unrealistic and dangerous 'ideal' images.

What parents can do

Parents can strive to ensure that at least at home their children receive the right messages. Giving reassurance that thin is not the most desirable option is an increasingly difficult message to sell young people, but a very important one. Strive to build up the self-esteem of your children so that the major focus is not on body shape or weight. This process does not happen overnight and is best established in childhood. It's never too late, however, for parents to help a young person to improve their self-esteem. Convince your adolescent to branch out and learn a new skill or join a sporting club. Activities such as these will often help shift the focus away from the 'body stuff'.

High achievers

Another cause of eating disorders in young people is thought to be overwhelming pressure to succeed or achieve. Red alert!

What parents can do

Young people need to know that parents are not going to dump them if they don't reach a particular academic standard or gain entry to a particular university course. Young people need to know that parental love is unconditional.

Perfectionists

Often, sufferers of eating disorders are perfectionists.

What parents can do

Parents can work to ensure that from an early age young children don't become perfectionists, thus placing them in a position where they are imposing enormous pressure on themselves. Help your children to put things in perspective. A young child needs to be guided and helped to be able to judge when a task is completed well. Keeping an eye on homework habits will soon show when a young person is worrying unnecessarily over a particular task. A school assignment need not resemble a university thesis.

Traumatic events

Some sufferers of eating disorders have experienced traumatic events such as relationship break-ups, family break-ups, the death of a family member or close friend, or even the stresses associated with adolescence. However, the accumulation of a number of smaller, stressful events can also trigger eating disorders. While parents may be unable to prevent traumatic events occurring in the life of their adolescent, they should notice when a number of smaller things don't go well in the life of a young person. These events may appear to be insignificant to adults, but each may be traumatic for a young person. Try to imagine the significance of these events from a young person's perspective.

What parents can do

Young people can be greatly affected by any setback, stressful event or significant loss. They often hide their feelings and parents can help by finding the right time to open up a discussion about whatever has happened to change a young person's world. It is extremely important to be aware of the feelings of a young person and to acknowledge them.

It is usually not helpful to tell a young person that disappointments and sad events are inevitable, and that they will pass. Telling a young person that one day they will look back and laugh, is not particularly useful. This kind of approach is more likely to cause a young person to feel both grief and anger. They sometimes simply need to know that their parents have noticed they are sad or unhappy.

It's usually not a good idea to force a young person to talk about a sad incident. If, however, parents do notice that their adolescent isn't getting over what has happened after a reasonable time has passed, then gently approach the subject. If the young person is still reluctant to talk and isn't returning to their old self, then take some action. This could be to look for someone who is a 'significant person' in the adolescent's life, or even seek professional advice from a counsellor.

Low self-esteem

Many sufferers of eating disorders have low self-esteem.

What parents can do

Parents are in the best position to ensure that from a very young age their children are given reassurance, praise and above all, the message that they are wonderful. Having a positive self-image before hitting the adolescent years is a strong protective factor. Listening to the opinions of young people can give them the clear message that they are valued members of the family. Making sure that young people know that parental love will never be withdrawn for any reason greatly assists young people to be aware that they are important. All of these positive messages help increase the self-esteem of a young person and decrease the likelihood that they will be so unhappy with themselves that they could develop an eating disorder.

The facts about eating disorders

- Approximately one in 100 adolescent girls develops anorexia nervosa.
- Anorexia has been diagnosed in children as young as seven.
- Anorexia is the most fatal of all psychiatric illnesses.
- Approximately 10 percent of young adults, and 25 percent of children with anorexia are male.
- It is common for people with bulimia to keep their disorder hidden for eight to ten years. Bulimics are more difficult to detect than anorexics because the former are often at a normal body weight.
- It is estimated that only one in ten cases of bulimia is detected.
- Approximately 17 percent of males are on some form of diet and steroid abuse, and exercise disorders are increasing in the young male population.
- Over 30 percent of young males want their body to be heavier and the same proportion want their body to be lighter.
- Eating disorders can result in reduced bone density, infertility, kidney failure, low blood pressure, hair loss, chronic fatigue, a loss of logical thought processes, shrinkage of internal organs including kidneys, heart and brain, heart failure and possibly death.
- Emotional problems associated with eating disorders are depression, social isolation, feelings of guilt, self-disgust and self-loathing, sometimes leading to thoughts of suicide.

Signs of eating disorders

Parents need to be alert for a number of warning signals that could indicate a young person is developing an eating disorder. Some of these are:

- Weight loss, preoccupation with weight and appearance
- Avoidance of meal times and other occasions where food is involved
- Excessive exercising
- Changes in clothing worn – beginning to wear baggy clothes to hide weight loss
- Mood changes, avoidance of social contact with others, fatigue, anxiety, depression
- Visits to the bathroom after meals

What parents can do

It is important for parents to approach their adolescent in a non-judgemental and calm way, but also to do something about the issue as soon as possible. The best approach is to give the message that the young person is loved and that the parent is simply concerned. Usually a young person will initially deny having an eating problem so parents need to allow time and space for them to be ready to talk in more depth. Return to the issue, however, and reassure your adolescent that they have the full support of the family. Persuading a young person to have a medical examination is a good start. There are organisations set up specifically for people with eating disorders and their friends and family members. Support groups are available where health professionals give expert guidance and young people can meet others their age with eating disorders.

Parents, teachers, society as a whole, need to address the message that 'Thin is beautiful'. Young people need to be nurtured and encouraged so that they are confident they are loved, valuable and talented. The secret is to find what lights up their eyes! Everyone is good at something. Adolescents with positive self-esteem are less likely to develop eating disorders. Fit and busy young people are generally happy.

Drug use and young people

While this is a very frightening issue for parents, it is important to remain calm if you believe your adolescent may be experimenting with drugs. To ensure you are able to protect your adolescent, arm yourself with information. Find a 'good' time and choose your words very carefully before initiating any discussion. First communicate your love and concern. Don't attack, threaten or blame. Say that you are there to support and help. Your adolescent may actually welcome the chance to talk, but is more likely to at first deny everything. Give a clear message that you care and are always there for your adolescent. Listen carefully and try to find out why your adolescent has used drugs: peer pressure, other underlying issues or unhappiness, a one-off adolescent experiment?

In general, young people tend to live for the moment with a frightening disregard for the long-term health implications of their behaviour. Despite graphic media campaigns designed to 'scare the life out of them', young people often believe that they are invincible. Some parents will remember the days when it was hard to even imagine being as old as twenty. So, how can parents hope to influence young people to be careful or to look after themselves when many young people feel that 'It won't harm me'? Perhaps the only effective approach is to make young people feel so special and loved that they will want to stay alive and well. That all-important connectedness can actually make young people at least hesitate and think twice about engaging in high-risk behaviour. It creates a protective barrier. And, when parents still discover that the worst has happened, the overriding message shouldn't be 'How could you do this to us?' but, 'Thank God you're alright! We don't know how we could cope if anything happened to you! Do you know how important you are to us?' Make the message clear and devoid of accusations, and focus on the fact that you love your adolescent.

A couple of ways to open up the discussion:

- 'Can we have a talk? I'm really worried sick. You don't seem yourself lately. There is so much being said about drugs. I'm worried you are upset or that you might be talked into trying drugs.' (Nice touch to ask rather than demand a talk)
- 'You know how important you are to me. Is it okay if I ask you something? What do you think about the whole drug issue?' (Again, good approach because young people hate adults demanding an answer)

Drugs – a mother's discovery

Two years ago my youngest daughter told me that her sister, Anna, was on marijuana. I confronted Anna and she denied everything. I believed her probably because I wanted to. I didn't want it to be true.

Just a few months ago, it hit me that something was very wrong with Anna. I suddenly realised she had lost a lot of weight. She came to show me a new dress she had bought for her birthday. As she stood there, my heart stopped. I can't describe how shocked I was. My God, I thought. What's wrong with her? She was a thousand times thinner than I had realised. My thoughts began to race … she always seemed to be sick with one stomach complaint or another … she was almost always irritable or anxious and had become very untidy and disorganised … her grades had dropped at school the year before until finally the school suggested that I find her a more 'suitable' school. All of this hit me in the face as I saw how terribly thin she was that awful awful day.

Anna was living with my ex-husband so, as soon as she left to go home, I started to put the pieces together. When I began to consider that she was probably 'on something', I was horrified. Needless to say, I didn't get any sleep that night and couldn't go to work for several days. I frantically rang numbers in the phone book for help on how to deal with this and how to approach my daughter about it. I had to have accurate information to know if my suspicions were right because, if it was true, I didn't want to risk my daughter denying everything if I approached her. I had to be ready to help her. I went to our family doctor and spoke to many counsellors. They were all very supportive as I cried over and over again. All of the reading I did and the talking with the experts confirmed that Anna did have many of the typical symptoms of drug users. Eventually I felt that I had enough knowledge to confront her and say that I thought she was taking marijuana.

Although Anna denied it at first, when I was determined to keep talking about what I had learnt, she finally confessed that I was right. I was lucky that the timing was right too because she had come to a point where she accepted that she needed my help and support. She did not like what was happening to her body and she was at desperation point too. I organised for Anna to go to our family doctor and also to counsellors who had expertise in working with young people with this issue. While Anna was ready for help, I was the one who suddenly wasn't handling the whole situation well at all.

I nearly died during those days. I felt like a failure. These things happen to other people's children. My daughter was too sensible for all this. I was angry with myself for allowing her to leave home and live with her father. I was angry with her boyfriend and blamed him for introducing drugs to her. I regretted taking her out of the strict private school as they may have been able to keep her on track better (even though they had suggested that she move somewhere else). I thought perhaps I should not have divorced, and that if her father and I were still together, this may not have happened. I began to blame myself for not making her feel close enough to confide in me. I felt that somehow I had not given her enough of my time and that if I had handled our past disagreements differently, this would not have happened. Most of all though, I regretted not handling the situation better the first time my other daughter warned me her older sister was smoking pot. I believed Anna when she denied it then, trusting that she would not lie to me, which of course she had.

A few months down the track I keep wondering how I could have been so blind for so long. I suppose I kept making excuses … I didn't want to believe it …

Anna still has a long way to go. We both do. The good thing that has come out of all of this is that we are now so much closer. We discuss everything and I'm much more open with all of my children.

Jenny, mother of two girls and a boy

Sometimes, no matter what we say or do, young people will still try drugs. Peer pressure is immense and adolescents love taking 'exciting' risks. But just because 'it will probably happen anyway' doesn't mean we stop talking. It's very important that young people know what we believe and how we feel. We must be well informed and able to communicate with young people. The secret is to make them feel so valued and loved that they won't want to hurt or disappoint us, and will at least stop at the minor risk-taking stage.

Before approaching her daughter Anna, Jenny spoke to the experts about drugs and their effects. She collected a lot of information and she knew what she was talking about. She had a plan, a strategy. Young people need to know we are prepared to fight to protect them. They need to have the message that no matter what they do, or what happens to them, we will never give up on them.

How would you know if your adolescent is using drugs?

- Marked personality change, enormous mood swings or explosive outbursts
- Impaired memory
- Changes in physical appearance or wellbeing
- Looking untidy, disorganised or lethargic
- Change in school performance or frequent absences from school or work
- Increase in secretive communication with others
- Increased need for money
- Withdrawing from interactions with the family
- Changes in eating patterns, especially eating less
- Sudden changes of friends and unwillingness to bring friends home
- Disappearing money and valuables from home
- Generally withdrawing socially

These may also be general signs of adolescence angst so parents need to be cautious before concluding that their adolescent has a problem with drug use.

Facts about young people and drugs

- Young people use drugs along a spectrum: nonuse, experimentation, occasional use, habitual and intensive use.
- There is evidence that 80 percent of young people will experiment with at least two substances by the time they complete secondary education. This might include legal or illegal substances.
- Marijuana is the most prevalent illicit substance used by secondary school students, with over 35 percent of all secondary students having used it.
- Harm minimisation education is important because young people need the knowledge and strategies to handle exposure to drugs. It is unlikely that all young people will avoid drug use entirely; therefore, it is wise to introduce strategies to educate young people about harmful effects of drugs, and ways to minimise possible adverse effects of drug use. Strategies include drug education in schools and early intervention strategies.
- Connectedness and good mental health will often prevent young people from moving from nonuse to habitual or intensive use. Being happy and loved protects young people, so keep those communication channels open with your adolescent.

Time out

All parents will occasionally need time out to be able to muster the energy to deal with the really serious adolescent issues such as depression, suicide, eating disorders and drug use. How will you recognise when you need that all important time out?

- You know you need time out when you can't remember the last time you were actually able to speak to your adolescent without the 'conversation' degenerating into a shouting match.

- You know you need time out when Neighbourhood Watch takes on a whole new meaning around your house! The neighbours really are watching – you and your adolescent.
- You know you need time out when the very sound of your adolescent's footsteps approaching your front door prompts your pet parrot to exclaim, 'Oh shit!'
- You know you need time out when you actually start to look forward to going to work and want to work overtime without pay.
- You know you need time out when your work colleagues send you 'Get Well' cards and, to your knowledge, you haven't officially been sick.
- You know you need time out when everything seems hopeless. You can't sleep because you're so worried, and you feel like running away to join a real circus.

One of the best ways to refocus and regain lost energy is to take time away from the 'frontline' and do something relaxing. From time to time, parents deserve and need a break – time to play sport, go to a café, go out for dinner. It's often also a help to talk to other parents of adolescents. Sometimes the grass isn't greener on the other side. There is nothing more comforting than hearing you aren't alone and that someone does understand. Time out is particularly needed when the situation between an adolescent and a parent is becoming explosive. It's okay to say to a young person that the conversation is over because everyone is too upset and the 'issue' will be addressed (not shouted over) when everyone has had a chance to calm down. Parents need to recognise when both parties are approaching the precipice and to pull back before someone plunges into the chasm. We all say things in anger that we regret at length. It's a good idea to allow time out for anger to dissipate and to reapproach the problem with lower blood pressure, lowered voice and a higher chance of resolving the problem with those you love – and yourself – intact!

> Parents are the bones on which children sharpen their teeth.
>
> **Peter Ustinov**

CRUNCH TIME

Respect!

How should you respond if your adolescent borrows your tennis racquet and brings it back damaged without saying anything?

- ☐ Ground them for at least a month
- ☐ Work out a way they can pay off the damages by extra work around the house or from savings
- ☐ Smash their favourite possession
- ☐ Say how upset you are and don't speak to them for a few weeks

Ground them for at least a month

Fair enough, but it would also be a good idea to talk about how this made you feel, when you have calmed down. Adolescents need to realise that their actions can hurt other people. This could be a good opportunity to communicate how much your adolescent means to you, and that you hope that you are also important to them. Tone of voice is crucial here. Young people quickly switch off if they feel they are being 'lectured' or spoken 'down to'. There are other possible courses of action rather than grounding a young person. Is a month a fair time?

Work out a way they can pay off the damages by extra work around the house or from savings

Yes! Young people need to learn to accept the consequences of their actions. Replacing the racquet would be a valuable lesson. It would be a good idea to involve your adolescent in the discussion of how the money can be saved. Once the incident is over and the racquet has been replaced, it's important to move on and not mention the incident again. Giving your adolescent another opportunity to prove they can act responsibly will be greatly appreciated. This is much better than putting all of your valuables under lock and key and bringing up the incident at every family gathering.

Smash their favourite possession

You definitely need time out! Sometimes everything does become too much to handle unless you have an opportunity to catch your breath and relax a little. Standing back can also be a good way to put things into perspective. Don't fight fire with fire – you'll both be burnt.

Say how upset you are and don't speak to them for a few weeks

It is important for your adolescent to realise that their actions have an effect on others but the best way to convey this is by talking. Breaking the channels of communication won't solve much at all. The house might be a quieter place, but rising tension levels will destroy any beneficial effects anyway. Always go for communication rather than the silent treatment.

summary

In case of emergency

- Try to remain positive, calm and constructive
- Trust your adolescent and involve them in any decision making
- Help your adolescent to learn to deal with disappointment and failure
- Ensure your adolescent feels protected and loved
- Be aware that eating disorders are often linked to poor self-image and traumatic events
- Be alert for signs of depression – it is an illness that needs professional treatment
- Be aware that approximately 80 percent of adolescents will experiment with at least two types of drugs – legal and illegal
- Take parental time out when you need it

CHAPTER 10

Frequently asked questions

This chapter covers the issues of greatest concern to parents: alcohol, smoking, television and the Internet, body piercing, fighting with siblings, bullying, family issues, loss, divorce and single parenting.

There are important questions that parents of adolescents often ask. Here are some of these questions – and a few thoughts you and your children might find helpful.

> There is nothing wrong with today's teenagers that twenty years won't cure.
>
> **Unknown**

Alcohol

Q. My adolescent is drinking heavily. What can I do?

A. Parents need to teach young people by example and to communicate their concerns about the health risks of excessive alcohol consumption. Parents also need to clearly present what is unacceptable behaviour and the consequences of ignoring these expectations. It is important, however, not to overreact, but to carefully assess the entire situation before taking action that could have long-term damaging effects. Many young people who do drink do not abuse alcohol, and many others experiment with drugs but do not become regular drug users.

A good start would be to ascertain why a young person is drinking to excess. Is the reason peer pressure, underlying unhappiness or a desire to be 'part of the crowd'? Parents need to reassure a young person that they are a valued individual, and the fact that alcohol can potentially cause so much damage is of great concern. 'We love you and don't want anything to harm you' should be the dominant message. It's important to address the problem but to do so by following all of the 'rules' for good communication with young people. Listen, don't attack, know the facts, and keep it short and positive.

Young people and alcohol

- Very high percentages of young people drink alcohol – more than 70 percent of 15- to 17-year-olds. The greatest concern is that many deliberately set out to get drunk. Binge drinking has become trendy with young people.

- Of the 70 percent of 15- to 17-year-olds who drink alcohol, one in five often has more than ten standard drinks, and more than a quarter have more than seven drinks. Such high levels of consumption pose a significant health risk, even for adults, and have wide-ranging social implications.
- Under the effects of alcohol, teenagers find themselves in situations of vulnerability to both severe aggression and violence.
- Teenage binge drinkers face possible long-term physical harm, particularly to the brain, liver and stomach.
- Approximately 28 percent of secondary students engage in binge drinking.
- The Elliott and Shanahan Research group notes that binge drinking is 'a routine and planned behaviour' among Australian young people. In other words, it is firmly entrenched in their psyches. In a Western Australian study conducted almost ten years ago, ten-year-olds were asked to name five Australian prime ministers and five beer brands. Few were able to name the politicians, but most had no trouble naming the brands of beer.
- In 2000, the Department of Health and Aged Care report *Developmental Research for a National Alcohol Campaign* surveyed parents' perception of and attitudes towards underage drinking. It found that, while more than 50 percent of parents acknowledged teenage drinking was a problem, they consistently underestimated the extent of the problem. These findings are a real wake-up call to parents. Teenage drinking is something they should be thinking much more about in order to educate their adolescents to consume in a safe and responsible manner.
- Alcohol is a heavily promoted product that is glamorised and not presented as a product with the potential to damage health. Understandably, young people often see alcohol as a ticket to a good time, a way to relax and have fun. Parents need to ensure that a balanced picture and the right messages are being taken in by their adolescents.
- Few young people recognise that alcohol is a drug and that it is possible to drink enough alcohol in one session to cause death.

■ The misuse of alcohol also plays an important part in the rise in teenage pregnancy, the increase in sexually transmitted infections, date rape, sexual assault and, of course, motor car accidents and deaths.

Smoking

Q. How can I make my adolescent give up smoking?

A. Set a good example and don't smoke in front of your adolescent. Better still, don't smoke. Try to anticipate some of the situations you will have to deal with. Your adolescent might admit they smoke. Thinking about this and your reaction in advance, can help you remain calm if it does happen, and help you to deal with it sensibly.

Because the media loves to demonise particular drugs and ignore others, we often forget about tobacco when we think of young people and drugs. We live in a drug-using society so the odds are that at some time your child will come across tobacco and try it. The good news is that there are protective factors that decrease the likelihood of young people continuing to smoke. Building up a relationship of trust and talking about your concerns will help reduce the risks of your adolescent smoking. Being well-informed about tobacco will enable you to answer questions your adolescent may have. Make sure your children know you love them, and will always try to be on their side, even if you do not always agree with their behaviour. They will be more willing to share their problems with you if they trust you.

If you are already involved in serious conflict about this issue, the more you make a fuss about it, the more adolescents tend to dig in their heels. Make it clear why you disapprove, and remember, you have the right to a smoke-free home. Passive smoking is a real health risk for people who live with smokers. Ultimately, if adolescents choose to smoke, then that is their choice, and they must face the consequences. A parent's task is to make sure that it is an informed choice. If a serious conflict develops between you and your adolescent over smoking, this may prevent you being able to share other issues in your child's life.

Sometimes it is necessary to consider a compromise solution such as allowing your adolescent to smoke in a designated area of the garden.

Facts about smoking

- It is addictive, toxic and ultimately lethal, killing millions.
- It may act as a 'gateway drug' or the first step to the use of other drugs such as marijuana.
- While as a parent you may worry about ecstacy, LSD, heroin and cocaine, you should know that tobacco is the only drug that kills one in three of its users (when used exactly as intended).
- Tobacco is smoked by over 25 percent of sixteen-year-olds across Australia.
- Tobacco contains three main components: nicotine, tar and carbon monoxide.
- Nicotine, which causes dependency, is a highly toxic chemical that can affect heart rate, increase blood pressure and decrease blood circulation. Nicotine is five times more addictive than heroin.
- Tar is the main substance in tobacco linked to cancer.
- There are 43 cancer-causing substances in tobacco.
- Tar is a major contributor to respiratory diseases affecting the flexibility of small air sacs in the lungs.
- High levels of the toxic gas carbon monoxide are found in the blood of smokers.
- Carbon monoxide increases the risk of developing circulation problems such as hardening of the arteries and coronary heart disease.
- More than 600 additives can legally be added to tobacco products. These include coffee extract, sugar, vanilla and cocoa.
- Cocoa, when burned in a cigarette, produces bromide gas that dilates the airways of the lungs, and increases the body's ability to absorb nicotine. Smokers soon become nicotine dependent.
- A young person who starts smoking at age fourteen, is five times more likely to die from lung cancer than someone who began smoking at 24, and fifteen times more likely to die from lung cancer than someone who has never smoked.

Computers and television

Q. My adolescent is addicted to the Internet and computer games. Television is also a real problem. What can I do?

A. Parents should not feel afraid to set limitations on any adolescent behaviour. It's a good idea, however, to have some reasons ready for what you will propose. If school work is suffering, for example, then limit the time your adolescent spends surfing the Net, playing computer games and watching television. Another good point to make is that the rest of the family rarely sees them. Outline set times when you expect the family will always be together. Having meals together as a family is often mentioned by adolescents as being very important. It may simply take a little time to re-establish this and other family rituals if they have disappeared because of busy lifestyles. It's generally not a good idea to ban these 'cyber interests', as any form of ban seems to enrage adolescents. However, negotiating limits on the time spent should be an option. Remember all of those hints about listening and respecting the views of your adolescent and being positive and reasonable.

Television invades your home

- Young people watch an average of three to four hours of television a day.
- Children average 35 hours per week watching television and playing computer games.
- By age eighteen, your adolescent will have spent at least seven years watching television!
- Many children now spend more time in front of a screen than in the classroom.
- The average child will see about 8000 murders and 100 000 other acts of violence on screen in their first ten years.
- The incidence of obesity in children has more than doubled in less than one generation and children who watch the most television have the highest prevalence of obesity!

Young people, computers and television

Many television programs and computer games popular with young people have a high level of violence. Research is clearly showing that extensive exposure of young people to any form of violence can cause aggression. Excessive exposure to violent scenes can lead to young people becoming 'immune' to the horror of violence and even to eventually seeing it as a way to solve problems.

A recent study by Assistant Professor Thomas Robinson at Stanford University's Department of Pediatrics, found that reducing the amount of time young children spent watching television or playing video games led to a reduction in aggression towards peers.

Australian Bureau of Statistics research has shown that children between the ages of five and fourteen now spend more time playing electronic games or computer games than organised sport, and more twelve- to fourteen-year-olds surf the Net than ride bicycles. Parents do need to begin enforcing acceptable standards, and time limits, on these television and 'electronic pursuits' right from the time their children are very young. Encourage your children to become involved in sport and other activities that are educational, motivational and require interaction with other outgoing young people.

Make time occasionally to be with your children while they watch television or surf the Net. If an unsuitable program begins, parents do need to turn the program off, and to then explain clearly why it is inappropriate. Young people often tend to exclaim that, 'Everybody else's parents let them!' Generally this is not true anyway, but it's not a good idea to say this. Ignore the comment and simply explain that you care too much for your adolescent to allow them to watch such inappropriate material. You find it offensive and believe that your family deserves better. There are also many great programs for young people and these can provide an opportunity for parents to show an interest in the world of their adolescents by occasionally talking about issues these raise.

Adolescents can be at risk on the Internet. Warn them about inappropriate sites and the possible dangers of visits to chat rooms.

Maintain trust by emphasising it is not that you mistrust your adolescent, but that you are worried about some of the dubious characters who frequent these sites.

Some families decide to place the computer in the dining room or main family room, especially when children are young. This allows parents to casually monitor what sites are being accessed and to establish expectations before adolescence begins. It's never too late to talk about your expectations and fears. Show you care and that you worry.

The good news about computers and the Internet

Many adolescents are more relaxed with the latest computer technology than their parents. Adolescents have grown up in a high-tech world and generally have no fear negotiating their way through it. Even very young children love to show parents their expertise with technology. Parents can use this to great advantage. Young people love showing that, for once, they actually know more than their parents. Suddenly the tables are turned and they become the teachers. Allowing a young person to show you how to do something they feel completely at ease with, can give them a great confidence boost. A wonderful by-product is that parents and adolescents can also often have a fun time together. Not only is this is a great opportunity to praise a young person, but it can serve to 'humanise' parents. Parents are demonstrating a willingness to admit they don't know everything. This may also make young people feel more comfortable about approaching parents for help and advice later on.

Technological wizard in the house

It's quite a sight to see our son helping my husband Geoff and I with his amazing technological flair. I say, 'Hey, Mark, can you see what's happened with this computer?' 'Righteo, Mum. No worries, Mum, I'll fix it.' He's only seven. We tell him he's brilliant. We say, 'You're amazing.' We try to support him in what he has an interest in.

 Sarah

Cleaning up their act

Q. How can I make my children clean up their rooms?

A. While there may be more important issues to concentrate on, it's often the small things that really grate – especially when there are a great number of them. Let's extend this question to address any behaviour you wish to change.

Calmly explain why you don't want a certain behaviour to continue and the consequences if this isn't taken on board. It's important to be seen to be fair and to make the 'punishment fit the crime'. Try to phrase this all as positively as you can. Rather than, 'If you come home at 3 a.m. again, no driving lessons for a week,' try, 'We really worry when you don't let us know you'll be home so late. I'm disappointed, especially because I've been spending a lot of time teaching you to drive lately. So, how about you get home at the agreed time and I won't have to miss out on being chauffeured around for a week?' An effective way to change adolescent behaviour is to be fair and to discuss sanctions with your adolescent. It's also nice to give a warning first and then to be clear about your expectations in future.

Here are a few more examples of reasonable consequences to consider:

Situation	Consequence
Does not set alarm	Oversleeps, is late for school
Does not study	Fails. You cut back on fun activities
Is late for dinner	Food is cold or all gone
Doesn't take care of clothes	No clean clothes to wear till this alters
Overdue library book	Must pay fine himself/herself
Misses curfew	Can't use the car, or no television
Foul language	No phone privileges that day
Leaves things lying around the house	Confiscated for a week
Fails to do set chore	No 'taxi service' till it's done

I HATE THE WAY YOU LEAVE YOUR ROOM IN A MESS... THE WAY YOU DRESS... YOUR LAZINESS TOWARDS HOMEWORK... YOUR MANNERS... YOUR BOYFRIEND ...AND I ESPECIALLY HATE YOUR EATING HABITS... BUT I LOVE YOU

TANDBERG

Fair go!

" A very despondent student of mine confided that his parents had grounded him for *a year*. I didn't ask what he had done to warrant this extreme punishment, but my immediate thought was that a year must seem like an eternity to this young person. (I was also conscious of the fact that I was going to have this disgruntled young person in my class for the rest of that year!) He had obviously made a decision *not* to do anything at school, and if his mood in class was a worry, I dared not imagine how thunderous the atmosphere at home must be. At the time we spoke, he had done three months of his 'sentence'. Things were not looking good! I suggested that he study really hard and make his parents proud of him. Had he thought of talking to them about how unhappy he felt? No way!

'They're always like this. They won't change after they decide something! I'm sick of it!'

This young person had seen his punishment as a declaration of war, and anger makes young people extremely clever military strategists. Unfortunately, the casualties of a war like this are often parental sanity, communication and the general wellbeing of the entire family. As adults, we all sometimes impose a punishment in the heat of anger and later on wish we hadn't been so tough. It takes real courage and strength to go back to a young person, talk about what has happened, and reduce the 'sentence' to a fairer one. This is a strong move, not a weak one, and most young people are quick to see justice and respond very well to it.

Erin

> Let us never negotiate out of fear.
> But let us never fear to negotiate.
> **John F. Kennedy**

TANDBERG

Body piercing

Q. How can I stop my adolescent from piercing every conceivable body part?

A. The last few years have seen an upsurge in the number of young people inserting pieces of metal into sundry body parts. Parents should convey their concern to adolescents. There is enough evidence to suggest that body piercing carries the potential of significant harm. If possible, parents should obtain information booklets from local health agencies so that adolescents have credible evidence of harmful effects. Doctors are unanimous in advising that a significant risk of infection goes along with all piercings, even those done by qualified people. In order to save money, some adolescents resort to piercing each other or go to unqualified people. If sterile techniques are not used, young people are at risk of everything from a simple infection to hepatitis and even HIV.

This is a good opportunity to impress upon your adolescent how important they are to the family and that you are concerned about health consequences. Have information booklets with you to discuss these with your adolescent. Good luck! Remember to weigh up how important this issue is in the whole scheme of things. Don't allow this to damage the relationship you have with your adolescent.

> And my parents finally realise that I'm kidnapped and they snap into action immediately: they rent out my room.
>
> **Woody Allen**

TANDBERG

Fighting with siblings

Q. How can I stop my children from fighting with each other?

A. This is a common problem. Adolescents are excruciatingly sensitive to any glance in their direction yet engage in a ruthless struggle for parental attention. Sibling rivalry is often due to competition for this attention. Fights are sometimes an opportunity to discharge hurt feelings.

At all costs, parents should avoid being seen to take sides. The time for offering sympathy to individual children is in private with each. Comparing and labelling children causes feelings of resentment and insecurity. Parents often unwittingly compare their children by saying things like, 'Your sister never spoke to me like that', or, 'Why can't you do your homework right away like your brother?'. Statements that compare only prompt envy and animosity towards the sibling in 'the good books'. Each child should be treated as an individual and each given adequate attention.

If parents model good conflict resolution, problem solving and compromise when dealing with each other, children generally learn these skills. Leave them to solve their own problems as far as possible. Unless someone is being hurt, parents should not intervene. If intervention is required, remain neutral. Don't blame one party and absolve the other.

Possible approaches

- First of all, speak to each child alone to identify their feelings and perceptions of the problem. Listen carefully to ascertain the facts. While there are always two, or perhaps even three sides to every story, in the end what is important is that the fighting stops. Call all children together, after listening to each, so that everyone can see that this is an issue that affects the entire family. The message to the group should be that the fighting must stop because it is upsetting everyone, and the house 'rule' is to respect each other. It is a good idea to make it clear that if fighting erupts again, all parties involved will be reprimanded regardless of who started it. Clearly state the consequences such as no special privileges for a week. As long as the message is 'live and let live or accept the consequences', the fighting should cease.

■ Strong, brief statements are effective. 'I won't let one person I love hurt another I love!'

■ Avoid asking, 'Who started it?' This question always results in a noisy, messy response because it is assuming that one child is guilty and the other is innocent. Generally, there is no such thing as an innocent sibling. Determining fault is almost always impossible anyway, and is not the issue. Young people need to learn to communicate with each other, to compromise and to negotiate differences.

■ Choose a quiet, fight-free time to discuss with your children the fact that you do not like becoming involved in their fights. Assure them that you have every confidence that they are capable of solving their own problems. Children can come up with surprising solutions!

> Children and zip fasteners do not respond to force ... except occasionally.
>
> **Katharine Whitehorn**

Bullying

Q. How can I protect my child from bullying?

A. All parents want to protect their children. If your adolescent feels valued, loved and connected to the family, this is a strong protective factor. Young people who feel this level of security and affirmation at home are protected because their sense of self-worth is not reliant upon the opinions of peers alone. They are somewhat cushioned or insulated from the hurtful effects of bullying. If your adolescent trusts you enough to tell you they are being bullied, they don't have to handle it all alone. Unfortunately, many adolescents are unwilling to confide in parents because they somehow feel ashamed of what's happening. Be on the lookout for signs of any uncharacteristic behaviour that may indicate your adolescent is being bullied.

Bullying is the repeated oppression – physical or psychological – of a less powerful person by a more powerful person or group. With bullying there is always a power imbalance. Victims of bullying can experience anxiety, insecurity, low self-esteem, sleeping difficulties, bed-wetting, sadness, headaches and abdominal pain.

What can parents say or do when they become aware that bullying is occurring? Advising a young person to hit back usually only makes the problem worse. The age-old advice of walking away and not giving the bully the pleasure of a reaction is also only effective in some situations. Parents should not underestimate how difficult this is to do. Bullying can be a terrifying and unsettling experience for even the most self-confident adolescent. If your adolescent attempts to stay away from the bully but the situation does not improve, it is important to contact the school.

Parents must insist that their children stand up against bullying and report it immediately. It is important for parents not to trivialise what has happened. Incidents that may not worry an adult can be greatly magnified in the eyes of a young person. Adolescents desperately want to fit in and to feel accepted by peers. To be ridiculed and rejected can be an extremely traumatic experience for an adolescent. Most schools have effective policies to protect students and to address bullying.

Parents can also assist their child by helping them to develop a social network out of the school setting. This will increase self-confidence and ensure that there is a support network of peers who can make the young person feel accepted.

An equally worrying issue for parents is to discover that *their* adolescent is the bully. Adolescents tend to model behaviour they are exposed to. Parents who show respect for each other and the ability to resolve conflicts in a nonaggressive manner are teaching their children how to relate to others. Parents need to assess how much they involve their adolescents in important decision making and especially how they react when adolescents disappoint or break family expectations. Adolescents should not fear their parents. Parents who rule by fear are themselves bullying. Young people who perceive that they are powerless at home, often subconsciously seek to balance the situation and regain some sense of control by bullying others. Once again, the magic formula of making your young person feel safe, valued and listened to, will reduce the likelihood of them becoming a bully.

Facing up to bullying

A young woman came to me having endured three years of verbal, physical and emotional abuse. She had been repeatedly kicked and assaulted near school lockers, had rumours spread about her, endured vicious name-calling and even received a death threat via email. By the time she saw me, she was suffering from a major depressive illness. She had engaged in deliberate self-harm, had suicidal thoughts and was refusing to go to school. 'Alice' had not told anyone about all of this for several years, trying to deal with the problem on her own. This was a mistake. Bullies thrive on secrecy and 'Alice' had inadvertently allowed the bullying to intensify and to reach horrendous proportions.

Initially the major struggle was to convince 'Alice' not to believe the lies that the bullies told about her. Over the years her self-esteem had taken a battering and this was affecting her whole life. It was important to rebuild her shattered self-esteem and help her become a more confident communicator. A lot of time was needed to teach her strategies such as calmly and assertively asking the bullies to repeat what it was that they had said, thus taking the power away from them. Armed with such strategies, she was better prepared to face the bullying. Alice was also encouraged to develop another network of friends outside the school. She joined a local drama group where she found some supportive and fun friends.

Many parents ask whether they should change schools if their adolescent is being bullied. If the school has been informed repeatedly and the bullying continues unabated, then leaving an adolescent in that environment is unwise and harmful. Students who bully also need help in changing their behaviour. Effective strategies involve parents, students and schools working together on meaningful policies and practice. Bullying is too damaging to allow it to continue.

Michael

Signs of a bullied child

▨ Changes in mood. Being angry, aggressive, withdrawn, worried
▨ Missing items of clothing or books
▨ Cuts or bruises
▨ Unwillingness to talk about school and often feeling too 'unwell' to go to school
▨ Suddenly wanting to be driven to school rather than go by public transport
▨ Falling grades at school
▨ Loss of interest in favourite hobbies
▨ Inability to sleep or concentrate, looking very tired
▨ Suddenly spending a lot of time alone and refusing to do things once enjoyed with the family

Facts about bullying and bullies

▨ Bullying can cause depression, risk-taking behaviour and even suicide.
▨ Victims are far more likely to be depressed than those not victimised.

- Bullies are often very depressed themselves and disguise this with acute irritability and aggression. Those around them 'cop it'.
- Addressing the depression many bullies are feeling will often cure the bullying.
- Parents who suspect their adolescents are bullies should seek professional help as this is usually the sign of a very unhappy young person.

Family problems

Q. I'm having marriage problems and/or financial problems. Should I discuss these with my adolescent?

A. While young people should not be kept in the dark, at the same time they should not be burdened with trying to solve family problems. Adult problems are for adults to shoulder. Young people should be treated with honesty and be reassured that the adults will handle the actual problem. Of course, if decisions have to be made that will affect the adolescent, it is always a good idea to discuss various options with them.

Many parents agonise over how honest they should be with their adolescent. Often, young people know much more than their parents give them credit for. Worried teenagers have highly sensitive hearing and usually realise when something is wrong at home. Young people are astoundingly perceptive. Avoiding certain topics such as the progress of a sick family member can often increase the stress for a young person rather than reduce it. The truth is less terrifying than the picture adolescents may have constructed in their minds. Honesty is important, especially during difficult times for a family. It can increase the closeness between young people and parents. You are extending to your teenager a very valuable message. 'I trust you and believe you deserve the truth.' This is an important message to give to a young person. Above all, young people need to be reassured that they are safe and that whatever is going wrong, a solution will be found. Another equally important message to give a young person is that they are not to blame for the difficulties in a marriage.

Divorce

Q. I am going through a divorce at the moment and I'm worried about the possible impact on the children. Is there any way to minimise this?

A. It is important to reassure young people that they are not to blame for the breakdown of the marriage. Some young people, especially early adolescents, come to believe that they are in some way responsible for the separation of their parents. It is very rare for a young person to disclose this directly to their parents, and often they live with these feelings of guilt for long periods of time. In order to avoid this unnecessary guilt, it is recommended that parents discuss this issue with their children in advance. A simple explanation stating that the reasons for the separation have nothing to do with the young person is usually adequate.

Despite the fact that a major developmental task for adolescents is separating emotionally from parents, they also need family stability. Separation and divorce fly in the face of this. As a consequence, many young people are often angry that, in initiating a divorce, their parents have placed their own adult desires and tribulations before their own. Parents need to be patient if young people display anger or uncharacteristic moodiness, as it may take time for them to adjust to a major change in their life. As long as young people are reassured that they continue to be loved by both parents, they will eventually overcome this difficult time.

A divorce often means moving house and a change to a new school for children. This can mean that young people lose friends at a time of their life when friends assume so much importance. Such a significant loss for young people can compound the other loss they are feeling; the loss of the family unit as it was. Arrangements should be made to minimise disruption to schooling where possible so that friendships can remain intact. This is a time when a young person will need support from their friends.

Parents should also ensure that the children are not torn between them. Young people need to know that while parents may separate, they will not lose the love of either parent. If at all possible, parents should work to maintain a sense of stability for the children. They need to know that they are still of supreme importance to each parent. The separation of parents is a time of real loss for young people and they need support and love from both parents. Many young people hide their unhappiness under a show of anger. Parents should be prepared for this possibility and approach young people with great patience and sensitivity. With that reassurance of continuing to be loved by both parents, the all-important sense of connectedness with both parents will remain intact. Parents who separate should not allow guilt to interfere with their ongoing care for their children.

When parents separate, children should not become missiles in a parental war. The worst scenario for a teenager is to become the meat in a very unpleasant sandwich. Asking young people to take sides, or playing one parent off against the other is a common ploy among hurt and grieving adults. This is very destructive to the young person. Involving young people in the 'dark sides' of adult separation is counter-productive to a child's efforts to establish their own separate identity and can be very emotionally damaging to them.

Meat in the sandwich

One young man I counselled was caught up in a war between his parents. In the space of a few years, he went from being a bright, sensitive and caring boy, to being violent, abusive and having a substance abuse problem. As the parental battle raged around him, he went from psychologist to psychologist, and was expelled from school after school. His pattern of acting out behaviour was a barometer for the family distress.

Michael

Feeling good

I'm fifteen years old, although my dad says I'm going on twenty. My parents are separated and I live mostly with my mum, but I see my dad practically every day. I am close to both my parents and, to most people's amazement, they are close friends. I also have one brother, James. Apart from the occasional fights, I get along with him really well even though he's only twelve. We stick together a lot. As you can probably tell, my family is very important to me and I hope one day to have some children and a family of my own.

Down the track – Lauren at eighteen: I will feel fortunate in that not only have I had two wonderfully supportive parents, but inspirational teachers, too – a father who has taught me that whatever I can conceive, I can achieve, and, my mum, who's taught me self-respect, allowing no room for me to doubt myself or her love for me. My parents are not perfect; however, they have given me the confidence to be proud of myself. By not forcing me to be the child they wish they had been, and by allowing me the freedom to learn from my own mistakes, they have given me the greatest gift of all – strength of will.

My stepdad is also an important person in my life. He has allowed my brother and I room to grow and he wants us to be comfortable. Recently I wrote in his birthday card that I love him for the way he loves my mum, and for the way he treats my brother and me. Ultimately, every child just wants to be loved.

 **Lauren Traugott**

A stepdad's thoughts

It's difficult to be a stepfather with your own children looking on. An issue that is constant for me is the guilt. It's unbelievable. I'm watching my stepchildren getting on with life, their house running along peacefully, while wondering how my children are. That's hard. I miss them. Then again, my stepchildren are also feeling the loss of their father. I was determined not to interfere with my stepchildren Lauren and James. The way things operated in my house aren't necessarily the way things operate with a new family. A step-parent moves into an established set-up – little things like who sets the table, who does the washing. That's a challenge. It's how to merge the differing opinions and views. But if I have a problem with my stepchildren, I go to their mother, not to the children. I didn't arrive telling them what to do. You don't go there. That's important. Otherwise their perfectly natural reaction could be, 'You're not my father. Get lost.' And they have never been hostile to me. They're great kids. It's about giving them a chance to adjust. It can't work any other way. I think the secret is to be patient and to let some things go. It takes time. Lots of time and patience.

 Steve

Grief and loss

Q. One of my adolescent's friends was recently killed in a car accident. They don't want to talk about this and I don't know how to react. What should I do?

A. If a young person doesn't want to talk straightaway, it is important to allow them the space they need. What is actually happening is that the young person is grieving and it is healthy to mourn a loss. Some young people hide their feelings for a time because they don't know how to handle what has happened. Generally they will need to talk after a certain period of time. It is a good idea to keep a close eye on a young person who has suffered a large shock like the loss of a friend. When parents feel that the time is right to talk over what has happened, it is essential to listen to the feelings of a young person. It is normal for a young person to be moody and to feel sadness or anger at this time. Acknowledge the feelings of the young person without dismissing them. Rather than saying, 'I know how you must feel', it is enough for parents to simply let a young person know that they are aware of how much they are hurting. Sometimes what is important isn't what parents say, it's simply being there through the very tough times.

While the loss of a friend or family member is acknowledged as a huge event in the life of any person, young people often experience other losses that can be overlooked by adults and can also be very upsetting for them. Young people experiencing one or a number of these losses may be at risk of depression if parents don't assist them to eventually talk through what has happened. While some of these events may appear trivial to adults, for a young person they may be extremely painful and are losses in the true sense of the word. Parents need to reassure their adolescents of their importance to the family and to ensure that the young person feels valued and listened to.

Losses that may adversely affect a young person

- Loss of connectedness to a friendship group because of moving to a new school, suburb, state or country
- Loss of good health because of illness
- Illness of a family member
- Marriage breakdown – loss of the family unit as it has been
- Break-up with a girlfriend or boyfriend
- Death of a pet
- Loss of a job – may affect self-esteem
- Unemployment of a parent – loss of feelings of security
- Failing to obtain a certain level of academic results – perceived loss of parental approval and love
- Not gaining entry to a chosen course of study – loss of plans and dreams and perceived loss of parental approval and love

Single parenting

Q. I'm a single parent and I'm worried that this will disadvantage my adolescents. How can I make up for this?

A. No parent should waste valuable time feeling guilty about their particular situation. A young person could be raised successfully by a single mum or a single dad, a grandparent, an older sibling, two mums or two dads, a parent and step-parent. As long as the formula adds up to a safe, secure and, most important of all, a loving environment, a young person has a home and a good family. Young people are more disadvantaged if they are in a very unhappy home environment. What is important is that they feel safe and loved, and this may mean living with one parent rather than two.

Sweet relief

My parents separated this year and it was possibly the best solution to an extremely traumatic and long ongoing problem. While many parents believe that they should stay together for the sake of their kids, it is not always the best solution. In my case, my parents were having serious fights over the smallest of things and the memories of all of those nights waking up to yelling and screaming still upsets me. Many parents assume that it will only be harmful to kids if they separate and they pretend that everything is all right. But children aren't stupid and they realise what is going on. I remember one bad stage a few years ago when there were fights almost every night and I would sleep with my headphones on so that if a fight did start, I wouldn't hear it. For me it was such sweet relief when I stopped being woken up at all hours to hear World War Three in my house. Now I'm living with my mum. My life is a lot better because I don't have to worry about my parents anymore. I feel like I can move on with my life.

Anushka, 18

Mum's cool!

There's me, my brother Angus and Mum at home. What's Mum like? She's cool. She likes all the same music as us and we go out together. If I have a day off school, we go shopping or out for lunch. If there is a movie that both my brother and I want to see, she will take us to the opening night and out to dinner. She has sacrificed everything for us. She helps us through hard times and is there with us during the good. Mum always backs us up in whatever we do and in whatever we don't choose to do. My brother and I are very thankful to have such a wonderful and fun-loving mother. Mum, we love you. You're the coolest.

Tegan McLaren, 15

Thoughts of a single mum

Raising two children basically alone for the last six years has certainly been very challenging. I have massive feelings of guilt because I can't provide the things they could or perhaps should have. Having said that, the children are far more self-reliant because they have had to be.

I have always viewed my kids as people first. We have babies thinking they will be ours forever. They do, of course, grow up very quickly. One of the most valuable things I believe I can give my kids is independence. It can be hard to let go and allow them to do things, some of which may, in fact, hurt them. Doing this, while still keeping them safe, is a bit of a juggling act sometimes. Some things can't be taught – they have to learn for themselves. I see advice as a 'guide', not as 'gospel'. This makes kids more aware of their decisions and the consequences. I have never believed in 'respect your elders' or 'Because I say so!'. Mutual respect is the key. It amazes me how terribly we sometimes speak to the most important people in our lives when we are prepared to show

TANDBERG

courtesy to total strangers. Taking the time to listen enables me to be heard too. Doesn't it sound so easy? I wish!

Coping now that the children are teenagers, one fifteen and one seventeen, has to be one of the most difficult and frustrating things I have ever done. Of course this also means it is the most rewarding and wonderful thing I have ever done. We have terrible rows sometimes, yelling and screaming – the slamming of doors. Boy are we communicating! Our best times, though, would have to be our 'video veg-out' weekends. We only leave the house to get more videos or more junk food. Usually both. We lie around in our daggiest P.J.s and watch our favourite movies again and again. We don't have to say much, especially during the movies. We just have a terrific time together.

I can honestly say that I really like my kids. I enjoy their company and I think we communicate pretty openly and honestly about everything. I'm not naïve enough to think my kids won't do things I don't like or approve of. But I do hope they are at least prepared and can make informed decisions to enable them to live happy, healthy and fulfilled lives.

 **Dale McConchie**

The best way to keep children at home is to make the home atmosphere pleasant, and let the air out of the tyres.

Dorothy Parker

TANDBERG

CRUNCH TIME

Alarm bells!

What should you do if you find drugs in your adolescent's school bag?

- ☐ Contact the school and teach your child a real lesson
- ☐ Contact the police
- ☐ Use them yourself
- ☐ Make time for a serious talk showing, above all, how concerned you are
- ☐ Ground them and forbid all contact with the friends you believe are to blame

Contact the school and teach your child a real lesson

The perfect way to alienate your adolescent! This will destroy any 'connection' with the family and is likely to enrage your child to the point where they will be very unpleasant to have around the place.

Contact the police

Do this, and you might indeed need the police! You will also lose the trust of your adolescent.

Use them yourself

No! You do need all of your faculties to be drug-free to be able to help your adolescent through a situation like this. You may need time out.

Make time for a serious talk showing, above all, how concerned you are

This could be an opportunity to really discover what has caused your adolescent to be in a situation like this. What has gone wrong? How can you help? Why does your adolescent feel the need for drugs? Peer pressure? Wanting to 'look cool'? Don't make this a lecture situation but try to encourage your adolescent to open up and talk to you. Allow the conversation to develop. Listen and keep the discussion calm and focused on the fact that you are concerned for someone you love.

Ground them and forbid all contact with the friends you believe are to blame

Because this is a serious situation, grounding isn't a bad idea; however, forbidding all contact with friends is a risky business. Friends are extremely important for young people and banning contact usually enrages them. Your adolescent could also interpret this as a lack of trust in them. In a serious situation like this, it's important to avoid alienating your adolescent. Give a clear message that you are there to do everything possible to support them. You are concerned and upset because you care, and you want to talk this over and do everything you can to make sure your adolescent is safe and happy. These are good messages that should strengthen the relationship you have with your adolescent.

DOUBLE CRUNCH TIME

Disaster strikes!

What should you do if your son or daughter is arrested for drink driving?
- Nothing! Hope they get time!
- Do everything you can to get them out of the situation and then ground them forever!
- Tell the police to throw the book at them to teach them a real lesson!
- Do everything you can to help the situation and then sit down and really listen. Find out what is going on and show support

Nothing! Hope they get time!
This might be a tempting thought, but you don't really mean this. You may just need time out.

Do everything you can to get them out of the situation and then ground them forever!
This is a situation all parents would dread. Of course you are going to support your adolescent but you also want them to realise how serious this situation is. Most parents would be feeling a mixture of relief that their

adolescent wasn't harmed, and anger about what could have happened. Allowing your adolescent to see what you are feeling is a good thing. It gives them the chance to see how much you care. It is important to calm down and then talk everything over with your adolescent. While you may feel like grounding them forever, do you really want your adolescent in the house all of the time? It might be better to limit the grounding time and to discuss ways that this situation can be avoided in the future.

Tell the police to throw the book at them to teach them a real lesson!

A perfectly understandable initial reaction. You'll probably get over it though and do what most parents do – everything they can to help. Talk things over with your adolescent. Don't let this incident put a barrier between you. This is a time when you can actively demonstrate your unconditional love. You are not going to walk away when the chips are down.

Do everything you can to help the situation and then sit down and really listen. Find out what is going on and show support

Yes! Your adolescent will probably expect to be attacked, shouted at, blamed, grounded forever. Take them by surprise and simply show how important they are to you and that you want to find out what has happened to cause this incident. Listen. Talk. Listen some more. Good luck!

CHAPTER 11

Final words and over to you ...

At the end of the day,
love is what really counts.

Ultimately, parents want their children to be happy, resilient young people capable of living life to the full and handling the knocks.

> **The best substitute for experience is being sixteen.**
> **Raymond Duncan**

What creates resilience in your child?

Over many years, psychologists have looked at young people who appear to have the odds stacked against them, and yet have made it despite adversity. They have emerged as strong, confident young adults despite being from very poor families, from war-torn countries or from gangster-infested neighbourhoods.

How is this possible? These young people share a number of key factors:

- They have access to a charismatic adult. This person could be a teacher, a neighbour, a coach or a relative.
- They have perseverance and the ability to learn from mistakes. They bounce back when things go wrong.
- They have a belief that their lives have meaning and purpose.
- They have developed 'islands of competence'. They know they are good at something.

How can you ensure your adolescent has all of this?

Access to a charismatic adult

Encourage your adolescent to become involved in school activities and activities outside school where they will meet role models who can inspire them. Young adults benefit greatly from having a mentor who can encourage them during the difficult times and who can help to build their self-esteem.

Perseverance and the ability to learn from mistakes

Teach your adolescent this from a very early age. All children will struggle in certain areas whether that be learning to throw and catch a ball, use a knife and fork or learn the alphabet. Parents need to show patience and to give the message that what is important is to try. Children usually don't thrive when the message, spoken or unspoken, is 'You are not good enough ... I'm disappointed ... (and, most damaging of all) ... I can't trust you to do anything right.' Messages such as these only encourage young people to give up, to avoid taking risks because of the fear of failing. Children need to be shown that parental love is not tied to any level of success or achievement. They need to hear that everyone occasionally falls down and that this is perfectly normal. No big deal! The important thing is to get up and give things another go. Parents need to work at giving this message to their children right from birth. Children with positive messages such as this are more likely to successfully negotiate the tasks that adolescence brings.

A belief that their lives have meaning and purpose

Parents need to demonstrate this in a million different ways. Young people realise that their lives have meaning and purpose when their parents take the time to be involved in their interests and praise their achievements. It's important that the young people don't feel pressured to be 'the best' swimmer, dancer, cricketer, runner or maths student. Parents need to make a young person feel proud of themselves and secure in the knowledge that they are an irreplaceable member of the family. Fostering that sense of connectedness with the family gives a young person a real sense of being a valued member of 'the team'.

In our busy worlds we often don't find the time to allow adolescents to spend quality time with the extended family and to feel that they have an important place in the overall family tapestry. Extended family members, especially family matriarchs and patriarchs often give young people valuable encouragement and are a great source of support. Young people need to know that they have a history, are part of the family and that their future is important to this group of people. They need to believe that their lives do have meaning and purpose.

Ensure they know they are good at something

From an early age, parents need to help young people develop interests and skills. Everyone is good at something and enjoys something. This should not be restricted to obtaining good marks at school. Parents need to ensure that their adolescents are not feeling that the only really valued achievement is an academic one. A valuable pursuit is anything that gives a young person a sense of achievement. The secret is to find that something and to give the young person genuine praise. Young people soon realise if praise is not genuine. They also need to be taught not to feel inadequate if they are not good at everything or not as good as others in some areas. It's not about being the best but about enjoying the process of being involved in life.

Fundamental to the happiness and resilience of adolescents is that essential feeling of connectedness to family, peers and school. Parents need to make sure their children know they are:

- Safe
- Loved
- Valued
- Listened to

Nothing is more important than this. However, if parents feel overwhelmed and are concerned that a young person is not happy or is exhibiting signs of being depressed, it is essential to consult a professional in the area of adolescent health and welfare. The wellbeing of a young person is too important to take a risk that things will sort out on their own. Signs of depression or unhappiness need to be acted upon.

Resilience in families

In the past two decades, many researchers have sought to identify the magic formula for **resilience** in families – those elements that contribute to family members' feelings of wellbeing, personal worth and general happiness. These findings are of paramount importance for parents of adolescents.

One researcher identifies three characteristics of resilient families: **cohesion, flexibility and communication**. All of these characteristics provide a secure and protective environment for young people to grow up in. Another research project undertook the task of identifying which particular qualities family members themselves saw as leading to family resilience. As high as 98 percent of those questioned agreed that certain statements were essential descriptions of **resilient families**. Some of these statements are:

- We feel strongly connected to each other.
- We allow each other to be ourselves.
- We enjoy simple, inexpensive family activities.
- It is easy to share our values and ideas with each other.
- We love one another.
- We often laugh with each other.
- We enjoy helping each other.

If parents work at making these statements apply to their families, adolescents will feel **connected** to their families, and will become much happier, more well-adjusted young people.

Clarifying roles

An adolescent is not:

- A slave
- A child
- There to fulfil your dreams and expectations
- Your entire life
- A clone of either parent
- A helpless creature needing constant adult attention
- Someone who needs to be kept tightly in hand until they 'grow up'
- A superior being entitled to anything and everything it wants
- A criminal requiring constant surveillance!
- Incapable of the power of reason ... given the opportunity

A parent is not:

- A slave
- Superhuman. Take time out when you need it
- A dictator who can choose the friends, clothes or career of a young person
- A helpless pawn in the adolescent hormonal black hole. You are allowed to set boundaries
- A magician. Sometimes you can't magically make your adolescent adopt all of your beliefs, so find a way to compromise
- The cause of all the 'faults' children have. Some they will acquire despite you and your efforts
- A jailer. Set boundaries, but locking young people up will not allow them to test the waters and to learn from their mistakes. Just be there when they fall flat on their faces, minus the sarcasm and the 'I told you so!'
- A money tree or an ATM – press the right buttons and out comes the cash. A better idea is to encourage responsibility
- A punching bag – physical, emotional or verbal. Foster mutual respect

- A nonperson. Parents occasionally deserve to have time of their own and time out, too. You are not simply a by-product of your adolescent's existence
- A doctor, psychologist or careers counsellor. Listen first of all to your children and then listen to the experts, especially if things are not falling into place despite everything you have tried!

The US writer Dan Kindlon says that the great irony of millennial parenting is that our success and newfound prosperity – the very accomplishments and good fortune that we so desperately desire to share with our children – put our teenagers at risk. The secret to great parenting is having an understanding of the developmental psychology of adolescence, how to use young people-friendly communication, losing a few arguments and negotiating on the others. Above all, parents should stand firm on any issue related to the safety of their adolescents and stay involved in their lives. Then, just sit back and watch the family grow closer.

Embrace the changes

One of the most difficult aspects of parenting is coming to terms with loss. The loss of that little girl or boy who has suddenly grown up. There hasn't even been time to prepare for the change. Perhaps, therefore, the essence of really good parenting is being able to let go. Letting go is incredibly difficult, and for a period of time brings a certain sadness. It's missing the child you once had and becoming acquainted with a whole new person. It's getting through those sleepless nights wondering if the young person you have nurtured so carefully is okay without you being there. It's trusting and compromising and accepting that your adolescent may not be emerging quite as you had hoped or anticipated. It's missing the days when you were listened to without question.

Young people do grow up all too quickly, but the good news is that there will always be a place for parents in the life of their children. Parents never become obsolete. And the best part of all is getting to really know how this new young adult thinks and feels about life's issues. It's sharing their hopes and dreams for the future.

Some parents love their adolescents so much that they want to lock them away from harm. They are afraid to show trust, to allow different thoughts and opinions. Caged animals may be 'safe' but they always appear to be so much less alive than animals in the wild. Young people also need to be free to be themselves and to express their uniqueness. And, more often than not, young people don't run wild when they are given responsibility. Generally they do measure up to our expectations. Parents who do have the depth of trust needed to allow their adolescents to be 'free', often find that they don't choose to run away after all. Home is a pretty good place when you feel trusted, respected and, above all, loved.

Our final words

Parenting is not an exact science. Every parent and every child is unique. The best each parent can do is to do their best. We hope that some of the thoughts and suggestions we have provided in this book will offer some possible courses of action and a laugh or two; never underestimate the need to laugh, the benefits of a sense of humour. There will be difficult times, frustrating times, times when it all appears out of control. Keep in mind, however, that love does conquer all. Continuing to communicate your unconditional love to your adolescent, especially through the most difficult times, will ensure that you both survive the roughest patches of the adolescent roller coaster ride relatively intact. At the end of the day, love is all that counts. We wish you all the best!

ACKNOWLEDGEMENTS

We would like to thank all of the parents and young people we have been privileged to work with in our professional lives. In many ways, they have taught us as much as we hope we have been able to offer them. We thank Rex Finch, Sean Doyle and Bryony Cosgrove from Finch Publishing for their wonderful support, suggestions and faith in this book.

Michael would like to thank his family for their love and forbearance, most importantly his wife Therese and sons Christopher and Rupert, who have provided him with some of the most important life lessons about raising teenagers.

He would also like to acknowledge the debt owed to Professor Sir John Scott, Professor Glenn Bowes and Associate Professor John Toumbourou for their professional support encouragement and inspiration over the years. Michael also wishes to thank Dr Michael Schwarz, Flora Pearce and Andrew Fuller, all of whom have helped him navigate the sometimes rocky terrain of adolescent clinical psychology. Lastly, Michael expresses his appreciation to the staff of the Centre for Adolescent Health Education and Training Unit for their help and support and to his students in the Graduate Diploma in Adolescent Health and Welfare.

Erin would like to thank her current students for presenting her with daily challenges, and reminders of how important it is to listen to young people and to have a sense of humour. She thanks her current and ex-students for sharing their thoughts in this book: Yanlo Yue, Nam Hoang, Alex Gooderham, Lauren Traugott, Anna Kelsey-Sugg, Natasha Stojanovich, Tegan McLaren, Anushka, Robbie, Katherine, Sue, Tim, Raphael, Jason, Michael and Amanda.

A huge thanks to the hundreds of parents who opened their hearts, but especially Androula Michaels, Mark and Helen Bourke, Sandy Lederman, Meg Robinson, Dale McConchie, Ruth Wallbridge, Anne Marie and Mike Minear, Dan and Nan Stojanovich, Adrian, Steve, Jenny, Ingrid, Sophie, Andrew, Peter and Sarah. Erin thanks the following friends and teaching colleagues for the interest and enthusiasm they have shown in this book: Androula Michaels, Serafina Ricca, Margaret Rennie, Lynne Robertson, Robert Lyons and Anna Antoniadis. Thanks also to Rachel Barbara and Bennie Mohammed from the Eating Disorders Foundation of Victoria.

Most of all, though, Erin would like to thank her family for the patience they have shown her as she has worked on this book. Without their support and encouragement, it would never have been completed. In particular, Erin is indebted to Nancy for her support and patience, her wonderful parents Marji and Peter, her brother Michael and his wife Lynette, her sister-in-law Gaye, and her inspirational nieces Carissa, Kasey, Demi, and charming nephew Adam.

HELPFUL CONTACTS

The first, and often most difficult, step is to acknowledge that you may need some help or advice to support your adolescent. Will anyone understand? Yes. Anyone who understands anything about parenting young people will empathise, so it is very important to approach the most knowledgeable people for advice.

Where should you go? Start with your approach local welfare and youth agencies. These will have staff who are experts in adolescent welfare. Sometimes local hospitals have adolescent units and social workers with a wealth of knowledge to offer you. Local councils and government agencies should also be able to direct you to helpful people. If you are worried that your adolescent may have a specific problem such as an eating disorder, depression or drug use issue, there are usually local organisations that can be quite easily located. Often the Internet is also a great source of information in order to find contact points.

Will you be judged as being a bad parent? On the contrary. Taking the initiative to research a 'problem' and to consult experts on adolescent health and behaviour simply demonstrates that you are a concerned and responsible parent.

Michael Carr-Gregg's *Help When You Need It*™ – using technology to attack a crisis in society

Help When You Need It is a revolutionary adolescent mental health package for schools, available as an interactive video on any computer screen. A major initiative of the Lions Rotary Foundation, *Help When You Need It* has over 30 individual video and multimedia presentations at three levels: for parents, teachers and young people. These explain how to recognise the signs of depression, eating disorders, ADHD and other mental health problems, as well as how and where to find urgently needed help.

It makes Michael Carr-Gregg available 'in person' to schools and individuals.

Help When You Need It can be obtained directly from e-Media Creation Pty Ltd, GPO Box 391, Hobart, Tasmania 7001, Australia
Phone: 1300 368 222 or (international) 613 6362 4258
Email: hwyni@emcn.com.au
Or visit the website at **www.hwyni.com**

AUTHORS' NOTES

Chapter 1

Page 4 Research from the United States and Great Britain ... – Herman-Giddens, M. E., Slora, E. J., Wasserman, R. C. et al., 'Secondary sexual characteristics and menses in young girls seen in office practice: a study from the Pediatric Research in Office settings, Network', *Pediatrics,* 1997, vol. 99(4), pp. 505–12.

Page 4 Every adolescent is unique ... – Melbourne psychologist Andrew Fuller has looked at this complex process and has identified six different adolescent groups, Stable Adaptive Functioning, Puberty Blues, Adolescent Decline, Mid Adolescent Dip, Adolescent Turnaround/Recovery and Stable Maladaptive Functioning. These are outlined in detail in, Fuller, A., *From Surviving to Thriving: Promoting Mental Health in Young People*, ACER, Melbourne, 1998.

Chapter 2

Page 12 Physical changes at puberty ... – Santrock, J. W., *Adolescence,* (8th edn), McGraw-Hill, Boston, 2001; Rice, F. P., *Human Development, a life-span approach,* (4th edn), Prentice-Hall, New York, 2000; Dusek, J. B., *Adolescent Development and Behavior,* Prentice Hall, New Jersey, 1996.

Page 12 A recent study revealed that, of the 14 000 children surveyed ... – This important research was reported in the *Observer,* 19 June 2000. Professor Jean Golding was director of the study carried out at Bristol University's Institute of Child Health. The development of 14 000 children was tracked from birth. It also found that one in fourteen eight-year-old boys had pubic hair, an indicator of puberty, compared with one in 150 boys of their fathers' generation. From a sample of 630 girls, one in six had started to show signs of puberty by the time they were eight. This is the first study into puberty to take place in Britain since 1969.

Page 16 Not only are young people reaching puberty earlier, but many are becoming sexually active at an earlier age ... – Lindsay, J., Smith, A., Rosenthal, D., *Secondary students, HIV/AIDS and sexual health,* Centre for the Study of Sexually Transmissible diseases, La Trobe University, Melbourne, 1998.

Page 16 Another consequence of reaching puberty earlier is that many young people question their sexuality much earlier than previous generations ... – This is very worrying because the research also shows that the earlier young people actually identify as gay, the more at risk they are of becoming isolated and suffering from a multitude of physical, social, emotional and psychological problems. For an excellent text that outlines these issues, see Remafedi, G., (ed.) *Death by Denial, studies of suicide in gay and lesbian teenagers,* Alyson Publications, Boston, 1994.

Page 16 Preoccupation with body size, shape ... – McVeagh, P. and Reed, E., *Kids Food Health 3: Nutrition and your child's development: From school-age to teenage,* Finch Publishing, Sydney, 2001.

Page 21 This period generally coincides with the transition from primary to secondary school ... – Hargreaves, A., Earl, L., Ryan, J., *Schooling for Change: re-inventing schools for early adolescents,* Falmer Press, London, 1996.

Page 23 Starting secondary school ... – For an excellent article highlighting the importance of school being a positive area in the life of a young person, see Glover, S., Burns, J., Butler, H., and Patton, G., 'Social environments and the emotional wellbeing of young people', *Family Matters*, Australian Institute of Family Studies, 1998, vol. 49, pp. 11–15.

Page 24 Does your child seem unhappy, worried or moody? – For an excellent article acknowledging the importance of parental participation in the process of ensuring that school is a safe place for young people, see Cumming, J., *'Towards Safe and Supportive Learning Environments: Strategies for Parent Groups and School Councils'*, Australian Council of State School Organisations, Commonwealth of Australia, 1996.

Chapter 3

Page 33 The importance of friendships – For an excellent journal article, see Meeus, W. and Dekovic, M., 'Identity development and peer support in adolescence: results of a national Dutch survey', *Adolescence*, 1995, vol. 30(120), pp. 931–43.

Page 33 One of the great risk factors that has been identified for drug misuse ... – Hawkins, L. J., Catalano, R. F., Kosterman, R. et al., 'Preventing adolescent health-risk behaviors by strengthening protection during childhood', *Archives of Pediatrics and Adolescent Medicine*, 1999, vol. 153(3), pp. 226–34. This study clearly indicates that young people associating with peers engaged in problem behaviours are much more likely to engage in the same problem behaviours.

Page 34 Searching for an identity – For an indepth look at various theories of adolescent identity formation, see Heaven, C. L., *Contemporary Adolescence, A Social Psychological Approach,* Macmillan, Australia, 1994.

Page 47 Sniffing out high risk taking ... – This research was outlined in an article by Rindfleisch, T., 'Kids sniff trouble' in the *Sunday Herald Sun*, 15 July 2001. A 1996 survey of school students also found that 34 percent of junior secondary students and 21 percent of senior secondary students had used inhalants. These findings are from *'School Students and Drug Use: 1996 Survey of Alcohol, Tobacco and Other Drug Use Among Victorian Secondary School Students'*, Drug Treatment Services Unit, Department of Human Services, Victoria, Australia.

Pages 50 Connectedness seems to be ... – Resnick, M. D., Harris, L. J., and Blum, R. W., 'The impact of caring and connectedness on adolescent health and wellbeing', *Journal of Paediatric Children's Health*, 1993, vol. 29, Suppl. 1, pp. 53–89.

Chapter 5

Page 72 To lead a psychologically, emotionally and even physically healthy life, adolescents have to successfully achieve four tasks during adolescence ... – Havighurst, R., *Developmental Tasks and Education*, David McKay, New York, 1972. A number of researchers and psychologists have since proposed variations of these tasks of adolescence. The tasks are therefore not rigid but tend to have altered slightly in accordance with changes in society over time, and subsequent changes in young people. We believe the tasks we have outlined are the particular tasks facing young people in today's world.

Chapter 6

Page 91 A landmark study of 12 000 young people ... – Resnick, M. D., Bearman, P., Blum, R. et al., 'Protecting adolescents from harm: Findings from the national longitudinal study on adolescent health', *Journal of the American Medical Association*, 1997, vol. 278(10), pp. 823–32.

Page 95 A belief system or spirituality as a protective factor – Eckersley, R., 'Spirituality, God, science and the future', *Youth Issues Forum*, Journal of the Youth Affairs Council of Victoria, Summer 1998.

Page 104 Patricia Hersch observes in her book on American teenagers ... – Hersch, P., *A Tribe Apart: A Journey into the Heart of American Adolescence*, Random House, New York, 1998.

Chapter 7

Page 129 Regularly give positive feedback ... – Toumbourou, J. W., Gregg, M. E., Davies, L., Carr-Gregg, M., 'The Parenting Adolescents Quiz: Parent education in early secondary school can be fun', *Journal of the Health Education Association of Victoria*. (in press) Michael Carr-Gregg's clinical interviews with Australian adolescents over the past ten years consistently demonstrate this phenomenon. Many young people are surrounded by negativity.

Chapter 8

Page 141 Research also shows that more adolescents today are having sex ... – Hibbert, M. E., Hamill, C., Rosier, M. J. et al., 'Computer administration of an adolescent health survey', *Journal of Paediatrics and Child Health*, 1996, vol. 32, pp. 372–77.

Page 141 the average age of first intercourse is lowering ... – Blum, R. and Rinehart, P. M., 'Reducing the risk: Connections that make a difference in the lives of youth', *Youth Studies Australia*, Dec 1997.

Page 141 Young people are tending to question their sexuality ... – Janus, S. S., and Janus, C. L., *The Janus report on sexual behavior*, Wiley, New York, 1993; Dusek, J. B., *Adolescent Development and Behavior*, Prentice Hall, New Jersey, 1996; Savin-Williams, R. C., *Gay and Lesbian Youth: Expressions of Identity*, Hemisphere Publishing, New York, 1990.

Page 142 There is evidence to suggest that the more parents discuss relationships and sex ... – Colebatch, T., 'Sex talks help teens decide when the time is right', the *Age*, 17 Jan 2001; Blum, R. and Rinehart, P. M., 'Reducing the risk: Connections that make a difference in the lives of youth', *Youth Studies Australia*, Dec 1997; Hibbert, M. E., Hamill, C., Rosier, M. J. et al., 'Computer administration of an adolescent health survey', *Journal of Paediatrics and Child Health*, 1996, vol. 32, pp. 372–77.

Page 148 Young gay people ... – Remafedi, G., (ed.) *Death by Denial, studies of suicide in gay and lesbian teenagers*, Alyson Publications, Boston, 1994. For other excellent articles and references, see Fontaine, J. H., and Hammond, N. L., 'Counselling issues with gay and lesbian adolescents', *Adolescence*, 1996, vol. 31(124), pp. 818–30; Feldman, S. S. and Elliott, G. R., *At the Threshold – The Developing Adolescent*,

Harvard University Press, USA, 1990; Hillier, L., Dempsey, D., Harrison, L. et al., *'National Report on the Sexuality, Health and Wellbeing of Same-Sex Attracted Young People – Writing Themselves In'*, 1998, Australian Research Centre in Sex, Health and Society, La Trobe University, Victoria.

Page 148 Fear being thrown out of home if they tell their family they are gay ... – In June, 1995, a Federal Government report, *Aspects of Youth Homelessness (Morris Report)*, was released after an extensive inquiry into youth homelessness. This report highlighted the need for special attention to be directed to four particular groups of young people. One of these groups was young people who identify as gay or lesbian. (Recommendations 107–11).

Page 148 Believe that suicide is the only solution ... – *Suicide Prevention: Victorian Task Force Report*, Australia, 1997. This report identified seven high risk groups, one of these being gays and lesbians, and concludes that the risk is 'particularly high for adolescent gays at the time of acknowledging their sexual orientation ... ' The 1989 US Task Force on Suicide presented more statistical evidence to highlight the seriousness of the situation facing young lesbian and gay people and it is likely that the situation in Australia and other countries would be similar. It was this report that found that as high as 25 to 40 percent of young lesbians and gays have attempted suicide, and that 65 to 85 percent feel suicidal.

Page 150 Young gay people comprise as much as 30 percent of completed youth suicides ... – Gibson, P., 'Gay male and lesbian youth suicide', *Report of the Secretary's Task Force on Youth Suicide,* Washington, Department of Health and Human Services, 1989, vol. 3, pp. 100–42.

Page 152 You are not alone. ... – The organisation Parents and Friends of Gays and Lesbians (P-FLAG) is now established in many countries and offers invaluable support to gay people and their families and friends.

Chapter 9

Page 158 Depression is the most frequently reported mental illness with rates having risen in the past ten years ... – Rey, J. M., Sawyer, M. G., Clark, J. J., and Baghurst, P. A., 'Depression among Australian adolescents', *Medical Journal of Australia*, 2001, vol. 175, pp. 19–23.

Page 158 As much as 18 percent of children and young people have been found to have mental problems ... – Zubrick, S. R., Silburn, S. R., Garton, A. et al., *'Western Australian child health survey: Developing health and wellbeing in the Nineties'*, Australian Bureau of Statistics and the Institute for Child Health and Research, Perth 1995, cited in Sawyer, M. G., Kosky, R. J., 'Mental health promotion for young people: A proposal for a tripartite approach', *Journal of Pediatrics and Child Health*, 1996, vol. 32, pp. 368–70. It is of concern this study also revealed that only two percent of the young people with mental health problems had attended mental health services during the six months prior to the study.

Page 158 Many adolescents suffering from depression are not treated ... – *'Suicide Prevention: Victorian Task Force Report,'* Australia, July 1997. This extensive Australian report clearly indicates that parents, and the community in general, need to be alert to the possibility of adolescent 'moodiness' being more than it at first appears to be.

Page 158 Young people who have depressive illness are three times more likely to use alcohol regularly ... – Hibbert, M., Caust, J., Patton, G., et al., *'The Health of Young People in Victoria: Adolescent Health Survey'*, Centre for Adolescent Health, Melbourne, 1996.

Page 158 Between 60 and 90 percent of young people who attempt to take their own lives have a history of depressive illness – *'Suicide Prevention: Victorian Task Force Report,'* Australia, July 1997.

Page 159 Young people and suicide ... – *'Suicide Prevention: Victorian Task Force Report'*, Australia, July 1997.

Page 160 Parents can help to protect their adolescents from thoughts of suicide ... – Resnick, M., Bearman, P., Blum, R. et al., 'Protecting adolescents from harm: Findings from the national longitudinal study on adolescent health', *Journal of the American Medical Association*, 1997, vol. 278, pp. 823–32.

Page 160 There is clear evidence that many young people who take their lives have left many clues ... – Donaghy, B., *Leaving Early – Youth suicide: the horror, the heartbreak, the hope*, Harper Health, Australia, 1997.

Page 161 Research now suggests that one in seven ... – *'National Survey of Youth Mental Health and Wellbeing'*, Australia, Nov 2000.

Page 162 For every completed suicide ... – *'Suicide Prevention: Victorian Task Force Report,'* Australia, July 1997. All statistics following in this section, unless otherwise stated, come from this report.

Page 166 What is anorexia nervosa? – Fairburn, C. G., Shafran, R., Cooper, Z., 'A cognitive behavioural theory of anorexia nervosa', *Behaviour Research and Theory*, 1999, vol. 37, pp. 1–13.

Page 167 Dissatisfaction with body image ... – Anthony, H. and Paxton, S., 'Issues in the measurement of body image and dieting behaviour in young children', *Body Image Research Forum*, Image and Health Inc., Australia, 1998.

Page 168 Media images ... – Research completed at the school of psychology, Flinders University, Australia, found that young adolescents are particularly vulnerable to media images of the 'perfect' body. Children as young as five and six were found to be aware of body image and to see dieting as a solution to weight gain. This research was reported in an article by Foley, B., 'Even the children think 'thin is in'', the *Age*, 7 Sept 2001.

Page 171 Approximately one in 100 adolescent girls develops anorexia nervosa ... – National Institute of Mental Health, USA, *Eating Disorders Publication* No. 94 – 3477.

Page 171 Anorexia is the most fatal of all psychiatric illnesses ... – Garner, D. and Garfinkel, P., *Handbook of Treatment for Eating Disorders*, Guilford Press, New York, 1997.

Page 171 Approximately 10 percent of young adults and 25 percent of children with anorexia are male ... – Paxton, S., 'Do men get eating disorders?', *Everybody*, 1998, Newsletter of Body Image and Health Inc, vol. 2.

Page 171 It is estimated that only one in ten cases of bulimia is detected ... – 'Through the Looking glass', *Newsletter of the Eating Disorders Association of Queensland*, vol. 3, Issue 11.

Page 171 Approximately 17 percent of males are on some form of diet ... – *Weekend Australian*, April 1999.

Page 171 Over 30 percent of young males want their body to be heavier ... – Body Image, *Issues in Society*, 1999, NSW, vol. 105.

Page 177 There is evidence that 80 percent of young people will experiment with at least two substances ... – *'School Students and Drug Use: 1996 Survey of Alcohol, Tobacco and Other Drug Use Among Victorian Secondary School Students'*, Drug Treatment Services Unit, Department of Human Services, Victoria, Australia.

Page 177 Harm minimisation education ... – Research into drug education led to the development of Australia's Harm Minimisation approach. For a more detailed outline, see 'National Drug Strategic Plan 1993–1997', *National Drug Strategy, 1993*, Australian Government Printing Service, Canberra.

Page 177 Connectedness and good mental health ... – There are numerous reasons why young people become involved in drug use. However, what the research is clearly showing is that family connectedness is a protective factor. Put simply, a breakdown in the relationship a young person has with the family, makes them more vulnerable. For more detailed discussions, see 'Drugs and our Community', *Report of the Premier's Drug Advisory Council*, 1996, Melbourne, Australia.

Chapter 10

Page 182 Young people and alcohol ... – *'School Students and Drug Use: 1996 Survey of Alcohol, Tobacco and Other Drug Use Among Victorian Secondary School Students'*, Drug Treatment Services Unit, Department of Human Services, Victoria, Australia.

Page 183 The Elliott and Shanahan Research ... – This was reported in an article by Hemming, T., 'Teenagers binge-drinking to drown their sorrows: report', the *Sunday Age*, 20 Feb 2000. Other nationwide research conducted for the Salvation Army by Roy Morgan Research shows that 17 percent of females aged 14 to 24 regularly drink 13 standard drinks in a single four-hour session. It warns that women should only consume four standard drinks in four hours to stay under the 0.05 blood alcohol level. Binge drinking among young males was found to be even higher than that of girls, with 20 percent of males aged 14 to 24 regularly consuming 19 drinks in a four-hour session. This was reported by Stone, K., 'New drinking statistics', the *Weekend Australian*, 7 Sept 2001.

Page 183 In 2000, the Department of Health and Aged Care report ... – *'National alcohol strategy: A plan for action 2001 to 2003/04'*, Commonwealth Department of Health and Aged Care, 2001, Australia.

Page 186 Television invades your home ... – A recent survey of South Australian children found that ten percent spent more than 1000 hours a year watching TV. This is more time than time spent in the classroom. Associate Professor Kevin Norton, of the University of Adelaide, found that the average child watched 630 hours of TV a year which was still more than half the time spent in school. The report also found that participation of young people in organised sport had decreased since 1985.

Page 187 A recent study ... – Robinson, T. N., Wilde, M. L., Navracruz, L. C. et al., 'Effects of reducing children's television and video game use on aggressive behavior', *Archives of Pediatrics and Adolescent Medicine*, 2001, vol. 155 (1), pp. 17–24.

Page 195 All parents want to protect their children ... – For a detailed examination of this topic, see Field, E., *Bullybusting: How to help children deal with teasing and bullying*, Finch Publishing, Australia, 1999.

Chapter 11

Page 214 One researcher identifies three characteristics of resilient families: cohesion, flexibility and communication ... – The work of American researcher David Olsen is discussed in more detail in Silberberg, S., 'Searching for family resilience', *Family Matters*, Australian Institute of Family Studies, 2001, vol. 58, pp. 52–7.

Page 214 Another research project undertook the task of identifying which particular qualities ... – The Australian Family Strengths Research Project is outlined in Silberberg, S., 'Searching for family resilience', *Family Matters*, Australian Institute of Family Studies, 2001, vol. 58, pp. 52–7.

Page 216 The US writer Dan Kindlon says that the great irony ... – Kindlon, D., *Too Much of a Good Thing: Raising children of character in an indulgent age*, Talk Miramax Books, 2001. Kindlon, who teaches psychology at Harvard University, talks about the modern-day dilemma of finding the right balance between helping children and overindulging them. He argues that parents who feel guilty about the time invested in their careers indulge their offspring by buying them computers, telephones and televisions. He says they compound the problem by shielding them from life's adversities – be they punishment by school or chastisement by coaches. Kindlon argues that this parental impulse to protect children from failure, pain and disappointment has crossed over into an indulgence that threatens to harm the healthy development of American children.

FURTHER READING

Anthony, H. and Paxton, S., 'Issues in the measurement of body image and dieting behaviour in young children', *Body Image Research Forum*, Image and Health Inc., Victoria, 1998.

Blum, R. and Rinehart, P. M., 'Reducing the risk: Connections that make a difference in the lives of youth', *Youth Studies Australia*, Dec 1997.

Cumming, J., '*Towards Safe and Supportive Learning Environments: Strategies for Parent Groups and School Councils*', Australian Council of State School Organisations, Commonwealth of Australia, 1996.

Donaghy, B., *Leaving Early – Youth suicide: the horror, the heartbreak, the hope*, Harper Health, Australia, 1997.

Dusek, J. B., *Adolescent Development and Behavior*, Prentice Hall, New Jersey, 1996.

Eckersley, R., 'Spirituality, God, science and the future', *Youth Issues Forum*, Journal of the Youth Affairs Council of Victoria, Summer 1998.

Fairburn, C. G., Shafran, R., Cooper, Z., 'A cognitive behavioural theory of anorexia nervosa', *Behaviour Research and Theory*, 1999, vol. 37, pp. 1–13.

Feldman, S. S., and Elliott, G. R., *At the Threshold – The Developing Adolescent*, Harvard University Press, USA, 1990.

Field, E., *Bullybusting: How to help children deal with teasing and bullying*, Finch Publishing, Australia, 1999.

Fontaine, J. H., and Hammond, N. L., 'Counselling issues with gay and lesbian adolescents', *ADOLESCENCE*, 1996, vol. 31(124), pp. 818–30.

Fuller, A., *From Surviving to Thriving: Promoting Mental Health in Young People*, ACER, Melbourne, 1998.

Garner, D., and Garfinkel, P., *Handbook of Treatment for Eating Disorders*, Guilford Press, New York, 1997.

Gibson, P., 'Gay male and lesbian youth suicide', in *Report of the Secretary's Task Force on Youth Suicide*, Washington, Department of Health and Human Services, 1989, vol. 3, pp. 100–42.

Glover, S., Burns, J., Butler, H., and Patton, G., 'Social environments and the emotional wellbeing of young people', *Family Matters*, Australian Institute of Family Studies, 1998, vol. 49, pp. 11–15.

Hargreaves, A., Earl, L., Ryan, J., *Schooling for Change: re-inventing schools for early adolescents*, Falmer Press, London, 1996.

Havighurst, R., *Developmental Tasks and Education*, David McKay, New York, 1972.

Hawkins, L. J., Catalano, R. F., Kosterman, R., Abbott, R., and Hill, K. G., 'Preventing adolescent health-risk behaviors by strengthening protection during childhood', *Archives of Pediatric Adolescent Medicine*, 1999, vol. 153(3), pp. 226–34.

Heaven, C. L., *Contemporary Adolescence, A Social Psychological Approach*, Macmillan, Australia, 1994.

Herman-Giddens, M. E., Slora, E. J., Wasserman, R.C., Bourdony, C. J., Bhapkar, M. V., Koch, G. G., and Hasemeir, C. M., 'Secondary sexual characteristics and menses in young girls seen in office practice: a study from the Pediatric Research in Office Settings, Network', *Pediatrics*, 1997, vol. 99(4), pp. 505–12.

Hersch, P., *A Tribe Apart: A Journey into the Heart of American Adolescence*, Random House, New York, 1998.

Hibbert, M., Caust, J., Patton, G., Rosier, M., and Bowes, G., *'The Health of Young People in Victoria: Adolescent Health Survey'*, Centre for Adolescent Health, Melbourne, 1996.

Hillier, L., Dempsey, D., Harrison, L., Beale. L., Matthews, L., and Rosenthal, D., *National Report on the Sexuality, Health and Well-Being of Same-Sex Attracted Young People – Writing Themselves In*, 1998, Australian Research Centre in Sex, Health and Society, La Trobe University, Victoria.

Janus, S. S., and Janus, C. L., *The Janus report on sexual behavior*, Wiley, New York, 1993.

Lindsay, J., Smith, A., Rosenthal, D., *Secondary students, HIV/AIDS and sexual health*, Centre for the Study of Sexually Transmissible Diseases, La Trobe University, Melbourne, 1998.

Meeus, W. and Dekovic, M., 'Identity development and peer support in adolescence: results of a national Dutch survey', *Adolescence*, 1995, vol. 30(120), pp. 931–43.

McVeagh, P. and Reed, E., *Kids Food Health 3: Nutrition and your child's development: From school-age to teenage*, Finch Publishing, Sydney, 2001.

Radkowsky, M., Siegel, L. J., 'The gay adolescent: Stressors, adaptations and psychosocial interventions', *Clinical Psychology Review*, 1997, vol. 17(2), pp. 191–216.

Remafedi, G., (ed.) *Death by Denial, studies of suicide in gay and lesbian teenagers*, Alyson Publications, Boston, 1994.

Resnick, M. D., Bearman, P., Blum, R. W., Bauman, K. E., Harris, K. M., Jones, J., Tabor, J., Beuhring, T., Sieving, R. E., Shew, M., Ireland, M., Bearinger, L. H., and Udry, J. R., 'Protecting adolescents from harm: Findings from the national longitudinal study on adolescent health', *Journal of the American Medical Association*, 1997, vol. 278(10), pp. 823–32.

Resnick, M. D., Harris, L. J., and Blum, R. W., 'The impact of caring and connectedness on adolescent health and well-being', *Journal of Paediatric Children's Health*, 1993, vol. 299(1), pp. 53–89.

Rey, J. M., Sawyer, M. G., Clark, J. J., and Baghurst, P. A., 'Depression among Australian adolescents', *Medical Journal of Australia*, 2001, vol. 175, pp. 19–23.

Rice, F. P., *Human Development, a life-span approach*, (4ᵗʰ edn), Prentice-Hall, New York, 2000.

Robinson, T. N., Wilde, M. L., Navracruz, L. C., Farish Hayel, K., and Varady, A., 'Effects of reducing children's television and video game use on aggressive behavior', *Archives of Pediatrics and Adolescent Medicine*, 2001, vol. 155(1), pp. 17–24.

Santrock, J. W., *Adolescence*, (8ᵗʰ edn), McGraw-Hill, Boston, 2001.

Savin-Williams, R. C., *Gay and Lesbian Youth: Expressions of Identity*, Hemisphere Publishing, New York, 1990.

Sawyer, M. G., Kosky, R. J., 'Mental health promotion for young people: A proposal for a tripartite approach', *Journal of Pediatrics and Child Health*, 1996, vol. 32, pp. 368–70.

Shale, E., (ed.) *Inside Out, An Australian Collection of Coming Out Stories*, Bookman Press, Melbourne, Australia, 1999.

Silberberg, S., 'Searching for family resilience', *Family Matters*, Australian Institute of Family Studies, 2001, vol. 58, pp. 52–57.

Zera, D., 'Coming of age in a heterosexist world: The development of gay and lesbian adolescents', *Adolescence*, 1992, vol. 27(108), pp. 849–54.

Also available from Vermilion

Ophelia's Mum
Nina Shandler
0091884152
£9.99
Women speak out about loving and
letting go of their adolescent daughters

**The Parents' Complete
Guide to Young
People and Drugs**
James Kay and Julian Cohen
0091815533
£8.99

That's My Boy!
Jenni Murray
0091889642
£9.99
A light-hearted yet thoroughly practical guide to raising boys

Trisha: The Family Survival Guide
Trisha Goddard with Peter Gianfrancesco & Dr Terri Van-Leeson
0091887704
£8.99
From the presenter of the top-rated morning TV talk show, *Trisha*, this
practical book guides you through the challenges, choices and changes of
family life

You Have to Say I'm Pretty You're My Mother
Stephanie Pierson & Phyllis L. Cohen
009188456X
£8.99
How to help teenage daughters love their bodies and themselves

Anorexia and Bulimia
Dr Dee Dawson
0091876524
£8.99

Helping Your Anxious Child
Dr David Lewis
0091884330
£7.99

FREE POST AND PACKING
Overseas customers allow £2.00 per paperback

ORDER:

By phone: 01624 677237

By post: Random House Books
c/o Bookpost, PO Box 29, Douglas, Isle of Man, IM99 1BQ

By fax: 01624 670923

By email: bookshop@enterprise.net

Cheques (payable to Bookpost) and credit cards accepted

Prices and availability subject to change without notice. Allow 28 days for delivery.
When placing your order, please mention if you do not wish
to receive any additional information

www.randomhouse.co.uk

INDEX

academic results
  celebration for 63
  disappointment in 64
  identification with 83
  parents' expectations of 59, 85
  and parents' love 24–25
  rewards for 62
acceptability
  by peers 73
  testing 21
acceptance of adolescents 62,
  216–17
adjustment, poor 65
advice, seeking 134
affirmation 74
age
  limitations of 51
  looking older than 18
alcohol
  abuse 182–84, 208–9
  depression and 158
anger 22–23, 50
anorexia nervosa 16–17, 166, 171
apologising 7, 91, 113–14, 126,
  132
appearance 34, 55–56
appearances, keeping up 16–17
arguments see conflict

behaviour
  consequences of 189
  middle adolescence patterns
    of 42–43
  modification of 128
belief system, need for 95–97
believing 120
belonging see connectedness
big questions, the 9, 21, 60
binge drinking 158, 182, 183
'birds and bees' talk 141
body image
  dissatisfaction with 167
  media images 168
  preoccupation with 16–17
  young males 171
body piercing 192
bond see connectedness
boundaries, setting 106–8, 112,
  117–18
boyfriends 79–82
boys 19, 171
brand marketing 13
bravado 67
break-ups 81–82
budgeting 78
bulimia nervosa 16–17, 166–67,
  171
bullying 195–98
busy, keeping 48–49, 53

career choice 82–89, 93
celebrations

academic results 63
  milestones 66, 97
changes
  adjustment to 65
  in appearance 34
  in behaviour 116
  emotional 12, 16, 18–19
  in life direction 60
  physical 11–12, 14–19
character assassination 128, 135
chat rooms 187–88
childhood ties, breaking of 21,
  22, 78
clothes
  as display of belonging
    36–37
  inappropriate 18
  left lying around 8–9
  'must have' 13, 36–37
  parents' reactions to 55–56
cohesion, family 66–67, 214
coming out (as gay) 149–50, 152
communication
  during conflicts 126
  emergency strategies 132–34
  establishing 124–30
  in families 214
  good methods of 109–11,
    124–32
  limiting 127
  and middle adolescence
    42–43
  non-verbal 127
  summary 139
  timing of 125, 170
computer games 186–88
computers, location of 188
conflict
  dealing with 105–6, 124,
    126–29
  defusing 135–36
  increasing 135
  between parents 204
  between siblings 193–94
confrontations 128–29
connectedness
  achieving 42–43, 50, 92–94,
    213
  and a belief system 95
  family 50, 212, 214
  ideal environment for 91
  importance of 64
  at school 94
  control, rejection of 40–42
  courses, choice of 83, 84
  criticism 52, 212
Crunch Time
  careers 87–89
  clothes 55–56
  drink driving 208–9
  drug use 207–8
  hair 55–56

leaving home 69–70
  messy house 8–9
  respect 179–80
  school blues 29–30
  setting boundaries 117–18
  sexual activity 153
  swearing 138–39
curfews 117

death of a friend 202–3
decision-making ability 84
decisions
  parents' 102–4, 109–10
  respect for 63
depression
  attributes of 157–59
  and awareness programs 165
  bullying and 197–98
  menstruation and 12
  and schools' role 165
dinner, family 112–13
divorce 199–202
drink driving 208–9
drug use
  broaching subject 173–74
  discovery of 173–76, 207–8
  facts about 177
  marijuana 158
  parents' guilt feelings 175
  suspicion of 105

eating disorders 166–72
education
  pause in 59
  tertiary 82
  see also school
emotional changes 12, 16, 18, 19
employment
  the first job 77
  opportunities 58
  transition to 66–67
  see also career choice
environment
  ideal 90–118
  supportive family 93–94
equality parenting style 102–4
expectations
  inconsistent 109–11
  modification of 114
  not reached 64
  parents' 59, 93
extended family 54, 212–13

fairness 107–8, 110–11, 114,
  189, 190–91
families
  close 66–67, 115
  extended 54, 212–13
  importance of 92–93
  meetings 133–34
  problems 198
  resilient 214

support of 93–94
fear
  experiencing 22–23
  of parents 62
fights *see* conflict
firsts, time of 66
friends
  acceptance of 33–34, 52,
    80–81
  death of 202–3
  during divorce 199
  high risk taking and 80–81
  importance of 33–34, 79, 80
  network of 26
  outside family 76
  parents' 53, 54
  parents as 206

gays
  acceptance of 145
  experiences of 148–50, 152
  parents' reactions to 150–52
  social stigma and 147
  stereotypes of 151
girlfriends 79–82
girls, changes 18
glue-sniffing 47
goals 82–86
go-betweens 132–33
grandparents
  experience of 3
  as sounding boards 53
grief 202–3
grounding 190–91, 208
growing up
  acceptance of 216–17
  signs of 60–61, 78
growth rate 12
guides, need for 52

hair 38, 55–56
handshaking 60
'hands-off' parenting style 104
harm minimisation
  and drug use education 177
  and risk taking 45–46
head-in-the-sand parenting
    style 104–6
health education 11
height
  comments on 14
  variations in 17
high marks *see* academic
    results
home
  appreciating 67–68
  living at 58
  supportive 93–94
  teens' ideal 93
  threats to leave 69–70, 130
homework 118
homosexuality 145, 147
  see also gays
hormones 12, 19
humour 34–35, 39, 54, 127
hurdles, early adolescence 21

hygiene, personal 11

identity
  confusion 73
  forming 73–76
  and parental help 74–75
  search for 32, 34–39, 58
  vocational 84
incentives to study 62
inconsistency 109–11
independence
  economic 82–86
  encouraging 54
  personal 76–78
  transition to 45–46, 49, 106–7
insults 135
interests
  academic 24
  challenging 48–49, 53
  development of 213
  new 66
  and occupations 75
  outdoor 48
  outside school 25–26
  parents' encouragement 26
  parents' knowledge of
    131–32
  sharing of 28, 43, 98
Internet
  confidence with 188
  monitoring of use 187
  sexual curiosity 141
  time limits 186

journey of life 20

kid glove parenting style 106–8

laissez-faire parenting style
    109–11
language
  inappropriate 14, 108,
    138–39, 189
  positive 52
latchkey kids 91
lesbians *see* gays
letting go 216–17
life
  basic belief in 95
  the big questions 96, 97
  journey 20
  meaning and purpose 212–13
limits, setting 106–8, 112, 117–18
listening 27, 51, 81, 93, 120,
    127, 134, 170
living at home 58
'loser' term 29
'losing it' 126
loss
  coming to terms with 216
  by death 202–3
  experiencing 22–23
  types of 203
love objects 79–82, 80–82
loyalty, family 100

magazines, sexual curiosity 141
marijuana use 158
marketing to adolescents 13
maturity
  acceptance of 216–17
  clothing and 18
  disciplined studies 84
  physical 17
  'pushed' into 16
meal times 92, 112–13, 186
media images
  of alcohol 183
  and body image 168
  pressure of 16
menstruation 12, 18
mentors 52, 78, 211
messy house syndrome 8–9
milestones, celebration of 66
mistakes
  dealing with 122
  forgiveness for 120–21, 123
  learning from 212
  moving on from 130
  sexual activity 146
money, responsibility with 78
moodiness 22–23, 159
movies and sexual activity 141
music 98, 117

Net *see* Internet

obesity and television 186
occupations
  apptitude for 75
  see also career choice
opinions
  differences of 27
  respect of 92
  value of 78
outbursts 14
overprotectiveness 76–77, 78,
    217

paint-sniffing 47
parental amnesia 2–3
parenting
  letting go 216–17
  a mum's perspective 6–7
  single 204–6
  styles 101–14
  successful 7, 113, 216
parents
  adolescents' view of 21–22
  emotional attachment to 91
  own youth 2–3, 44, 67, 122
  pushy 93
  roles 215–16
  shared interests 28, 43, 98
  survival tips 28, 52–53,
    66–68, 114–16
passions *see* interests
past behaviour
  digging up 123, 130
  parents' 2–3, 44, 67, 122
peace offerings 132
peer groups, importance of 79

peer pressure 142, 153–54, 182
perfect parenting style 111–14
perseverance 212
personal attacks 128, 135
P-FLAG (Parents and Friends of
    Lesbians and Gays) 150, 152
physical changes 12, 14–19
planning for the future 82–86
positive feedback 129, 212
positive outlook 95–97
praise 129, 213
pregnancy 146
pride
    expression of 61, 63, 64
    in self 212
privacy 100, 115–16, 137, 144
protective factors
    belief system 95–97
    family 91, 92–93, 98
    list of 99
    school 94
    a significant person 98
    spirituality 95–97
puberty 4, 11–12, 15
punishment
    appropriate 189
    unfair 190–91
put-downs 36–37, 38–39,
    127–28, 135, 212

quality time 34–35, 115, 212

recognition by parents 97
rejection of parents 40–42
relationships
    advice about 145
    break-up of 81–82
    discussion about 142–44
    outside families 79–82
    summary checklist 154
resilience 211, 214
resolution of issues 127
respect
    for family members 107
    lack of 179–80
    mutual 63, 205
    from parents 100
responsibility
    independence and 77
    money and 78
risk factors 100
risk-taking behaviour
    bullying and 197–98
    healthy 45
    high level 47–49, 80–81, 109
    low level 46
    responding to 47–49
    as testing process 44–51
    young gays 150
rites of passage 97
ritual 97
role models 211
roles
    of adolescents 215
    of parents 215–16
roller coaster ride 4–5

rooms
    searching 137
    untidy 8–9, 117, 136, 189

same-sex experiences 147,
    150–51
sarcasm 127–28
school
    hatred of 29–30
    leaving 61, 66
    parents' expectations 24–25
    parents' interest in 23–24
    as protective factor 94
    starting 23–25
school results see academic
    results
self-esteem, low 170–71
sensitivity 40–41
sex, discussions about 142,
    143–44
sex education 11, 141, 154
sexual activity
    discussions about 153–54
    early 16, 141–42
    media pressure and 141
    parents' reactions to 146
    peer pressure and 142, 153–54
    summary checklist 154
    unsafe 158
    worst case scenarios 146
sexuality
    discussions about 143–44
    parents' reactions to 152
    questioning 16, 147, 150–51
    summary checklist 154
sexually transmitted diseases
    146
siblings
    comparison of 193
    rivalry 193–94
significant person 52, 98
silent treatment 180
single parenting 204–6
skills 75, 213
sleeping over 144
smoking 184–85
sniffing 47
sorry, saying 7, 91, 113–14, 126,
    132
Spanish Inquisition parenting
    style 108–9
spirituality 95–97
sports 48–49, 187
stability 52, 199–200
stages of adolescence 1–9, 32
step-parents 201, 202
study
    course choices 83, 84
    incentives to 62
suicide
    contributory factors 159–61,
        164
    facts about 161–62
    gays and 148
    media influence on 159–60
    prevention 162–65

rates of 161, 162
    tendency to 160–61, 163–64
    unsuccessful 162
    young gays 150
support
    in early adolescence 26–27
    for parents 53
    rejection of 40–42
    unconditional 58–59
    survival tips 28, 52–53, 114–16
swearing 108, 138–39, 189

talking see communication
tasks of adolescence 72–86
teachers
    adolescents as 188
    emotional attachment to 91
    teasing 17
technology, adolescents'
    advantage with 188
television, impact of 141, 186–88
temperament
    changes in 157–58
    differences in 40–41
    and risk-taking behaviour
        48–49
tertiary studies 82
testosterone 19
thinking, development of
    21–22, 67–68
threats 130
time out
    adolescents' 14
    parents' 53, 127, 156, 177–78
time span of adolescence 4
traumatic events
    eating disorders 169–70
    suicide 164
    types of loss 203
trust
    child's judgement 54
    independence and 77, 78
    lack of 108–9, 120–21, 137, 212
    need for 122–23
    responsibility and 51
    showing 48

ultimatums 128–29
unemployment 82
unsafe sexual practices 158
unsafe situations 145
untidiness 8–9, 189

violence on television 186, 187
vocational decisions see career
    choice
voice, breaking of 19

weight
    comments on 14
    obsession about 167
    statistics on control of 167
    television and 186

youth suicides see suicide